Rodin

Later Drawings

Plaster cast of *Monument to Rodin*, 1910, by Antoine Bourdelle.

Later Drawings

With Interpretations by
Antoine Bourdelle

Text and translations by
Elisabeth Chase Geissbuhler

Beacon Press   Boston

First published by Beacon Press in 1963

Copyright © 1963 by Elisabeth Chase Geissbuhler

Library of Congress catalog card number: 63-11390

Published simultaneously in Canada by
S. J. Reginald Saunders & Co., Ltd., Toronto

Printed in the United States of America

Your study of the drawings, which is a companion piece to your study of the sculpture for Vélizy, might, flatteringly for me, appear at the head of an edition of my drawings.

(Letter from Rodin to Bourdelle)

Contents

Foreword

That Rodin was a great sculptor – the greatest since Michelangelo – is a generally accepted opinion which it would be perverse to dispute. That he has another and different claim to our attention is persuasively argued by the author of this volume. Only a relatively small number of the thousands of drawings in pencil, ink, watercolor and wash that Rodin made in the last years of his life have been illustrated or exhibited, and it has usually been assumed, even by those directly concerned with the subject, that such drawings were in some manner ancillary to the sculpture. Mrs. Geissbuhler shows in her book that this is a misconception. The drawings exist in their own right, as independent works of art, and though only an artist of Rodin's sculptural experience could have conceived them and given them their particular quality, this quality is essentially linear or graphic. One can best appreciate them by momentarily forgetting about all the great monumental works that preceded them.

Rodin, like most sculptors, used working-drawings all his life, but suddenly, when already an old man, he was seized by a sacred rage, a passionate desire to understand and depict the female body in all its subtle variations of gesture, movement and stance. Nothing is more moving in this account of his obsession than his pursuit to Marseille of a troupe of Cambodian dancers who had come to Paris in 1906 to give two performances. Rodin tells us that he followed them so that he could make drawings of them up to the last moment of their visit. "I contemplated them in ecstacy. . . . When they were gone I was in cold and darkness. I thought they had carried away the beauty of the world. I followed them to Marseille; I would have followed them to Cairo." These are the words of a visionary to whom a revelation has been given, a revelation of the deepest secrets of Nature, which are always secrets of form.

Mrs. Geissbuhler's book has a second purpose, which is to tell the story of a great friendship, the friendship of a master for his pupil, of a pupil for his master. Bourdelle, who came to Rodin as a humble assistant, was himself to become a great sculptor, but so long as Rodin was alive, he subordinated his own ambitions to the service of his master, and gave his master what so few of his contemporaries could give, perfect understanding. Particularly an understanding of these drawings "anthems in the light, flowers of science" – he recorded his impressions in many beautiful metaphors, of which a great poet might be jealous. Let the reader turn to the last section of Bourdelle's *Notes on Rodin's Drawings*, which Mrs. Geissbuhler has rescued from oblivion. It describes "that most intimate drawing," the drawing of a young girl; the description is a prose poem of great beauty, a beautiful poem that defines beauty itself. In the article on the drawings which Bourdelle wrote for *La Grande Revue* there is a sentence to which I would like to call attention because it reveals the secret of all great art: "This art advances from the fevers of the flesh to their geometric repose, and the first are so well enshrined in the second that their union is ineffable – ineffable by the sense of humanity which is equalled here by a sense of eternity" – a sentence that reminds me of Ruskin's definition of the greatest art. He also was writing about a sculptor, Jacopo della Quercia, whose tomb of Ilaria del Caretto in Lucca Cathedral, he said, "unites in perfect and errorless balance the softest mysteries of emotion with the implacable severities of science."

Mrs. Geissbuhler has very sensitively traced the relationship between these two great artists, and by doing so has increased the stature of them both. But the more specific purpose of her book was to throw light on a neglected aspect of Rodin's genius, and now for the first time the man and his work can be seen in that "wholeness" which for Rodin himself was the final quality of human perfection.

HERBERT READ

January 2, 1963

Illustrations

The drawings are listed as they appear in the text accompanied by the name of the donor and the museum to which each now belongs.

The captions (not repeated here) are for the most part quotations from Bourdelle's or Rodin's texts. They are offered as appropriate to the drawings, not as fixed titles, but as suggestions of ways in which the reader may see the drawings for himself.

1 | "Truthful Works Are Not Understood"

THE LATE works of a great artist, frequently the highest expression of himself, are often the last to be understood and appreciated. It is generally remembered that the year 1900 was a climax for Rodin's most celebrated works of sculpture, but it is usually forgotten that the same year was also a beginning for his genius in another field.

With his famous and most massive sculpture completed and acclaimed at the Paris World's Fair of 1900, Rodin chose the most supple and the least ponderous of media for the summing up of his wisdom. It was then, with as much love and power as ever he gave to his mightiest sculpture, that he resumed his drawing from nature.

The hostility, ridicule and even charges of obscenity with which these later life-drawings were received never interrupted the flow of their creation. The 5,800 drawings at the Paris Rodin Museum alone prove that Rodin drew almost every day to the end of his productive life. But the absence of understanding encountered by his drawings did wring from him the distress call which he addressed to his younger friend and collaborator, Antoine Bourdelle: *"Bourdelle, on ne comprend pas mes dessins, écrivez donc ce que vous pensez à leur sujet."* [Bourdelle, they don't understand my drawings, so write what you think about them.]

Rodin's complaint and his underlined, encircled request to Bourdelle is followed by this comment from Bourdelle: *"On ne comprend pas les oeuvres justes et les fervents de Rodin, célèbre dans l'Europe aujourd'hui, font tous acte de foi mais non acte d'initié."*[1] [Truthful works are not understood and the admirers of Rodin, who is famous today throughout Europe, offer him acts of faith but not the understanding of initiates.]

Bourdelle was the first initiate, the one chosen by Rodin himself to interpret his intentions in these drawings. Twenty-one years Rodin's junior (he was born October 30, 1861, in Montauban, France), Bourdelle became during the 1920s a sculptor and teacher almost as famous. To the ever increasing number of students who came from nearly all countries of Europe, America and even Asia, bringing Rodin their efforts, he most often said, *"Faites plus petit et plus intime"*[2] [make it smaller and more intimate], leaving Bourdelle to carry on. No wonder many stayed to work in Bourdelle's studios.

This association with Rodin as teacher, which began in 1901, and Bourdelle's fifteen years of carving for him – for Rodin was not a carver – made Bourdelle the ideal interpreter of Rodin's late drawings. The Rodin-Bourdelle correspondence shows that Bourdelle's gift to the master was an appreciation of his drawing based on real understanding unique at that time.

In all the many documents of the Rodin-Bourdelle relationship – documents which date from 1893 and which were added to by Bourdelle ten years after Rodin's death, and which cover a period of thirty-five years – the earliest mention of Bourdelle's connection with Rodin's *drawing* is a letter written in 1903. In that letter Rodin, speaking only of his later drawings, informs Bourdelle, *"Mes dessins sont le résultat de ma sculpture."*[3] [My drawings are the result of my sculpture.]

PLATE 1. Model for the *Gates of Hell*

This is third among the early models made around 1881 for Rodin's *Gates of Hell*. It is conceived as Rodin understood the cathedrals to have been, as orchestrations of beautiful blond and dark shadows. The following, from a letter to Bourdelle describing the Cathedral of Le Mans, might have been written of this model for Rodin's *Gates*:

Is it not the degree of light which gives all this coordinated energy? This energy passed into habit is eloquence itself.

Courtesy of the Caisse Nationale des Monuments Historiques, Grand Palais, Paris

PLATE 1

3

PLATE 2. *Adoration*

Drawn on ruled copybook paper with a wash of muted blue gouache as background, this is one of the anatomical pen-and-ink drawings of Rodin's Dantesque period. In the upper left corner there is a primitive sketch of the *Gates of Hell* as they appear in the early clay and plaster models. This sketch within the drawing indicates the exact point on the early version of the *Gates* at which Rodin apparently planned to place this group. The unsigned, undated drawings of this type were made between 1870 and 1890.

The Fogg Art Museum, Harvard University

4

PLATE 2

5

2 | Early Drawings

A GLANCE at the history of Rodin's drawings prior to the later life drawings which are the subject of this study shows that he had drawn for many years before knowing what it was to be a sculptor. His first drawings, as far back as he could remember, were his copies of illustrated pages used to wrap the groceries his mother brought home. Next were his drawings of natural forms, plants, rocks and the like.[1] At *La Petite Ecole*, as the School of Decorative and Applied Arts was called when Rodin was a student there from 1854–1857, he first discovered clay modeling at the age of fifteen. There his drawings must have been principally from plaster casts, for no living models were provided.

Urged on by a longing to draw from life, Rodin tried again and again between 1860 and 1862 to enter the National Beaux-Arts School. Even then, aged twenty to twenty-two, he knew his abilities equaled those of any other candidate, but he lacked the academic formula; nor did he wish to acquire it. Describing his experience forty years later, he said: *"Je me présentai à l'Ecole des Beaux-Arts où l'on travaillait d'après nature tous les jours de 4 à 6 hrs. Je fis trois fois les concours d'entrée. Je fus toujours refusé."*[2] [I applied to the Beaux-Arts School where students worked from nature every day from 4 to 6. I took the entrance examinations three times. I was always refused.]

The emphasis of these few lines makes it clear that the misfortune to such a poor boy as Rodin in being refused was the loss of an opportunity to work from life. Luckily, he soon discovered the free drawing classes at the Gobelin Tapestry Works, where as one of sixty students he drew from a living model for the first time and made the thirteen academic life studies preserved today at the Paris Rodin Museum.

During 1864 a few corrections in drawing as well as in modeling by sculptor Antoine Louis Barye completed Rodin's formal art school education. Privately, between his work for other sculptors, he was always drawing in any free moment and on any scrap of paper that came to hand. In Brussels from 1871 to 1877, the trees of the Groenendaël forest served him as models, and after his return to Paris, at the Sèvres Porcelain Factory from 1879 to 1882, he was sometimes allowed a living model for his drawings (he was the only employee of that establishment so privileged).

But most of his drawings of the years 1870 to 1890 were from imagination and memory, inspired by his reading. Léon Maillard has written that by 1878, Rodin had begun his long study of Dante's *Divine Comedy*.[3] This reading, with that of works by Victor Hugo and Baudelaire, brought order to the young sculptor's thoughts and emotions, as one sees them mirrored in his imaginative drawings of the next twelve years. And it was the "Inferno" that from 1880, if not earlier, supplied the frame for all Rodin's art during the following decade.

In the summer of 1880, when the French Ministry of Beaux-Arts offered Rodin the commission of a bronze door for the proposed Decorative Arts Museum, his choice of subject was Dante's *Gates of Hell* (Plate 1). He said he chose the "Inferno" as the subject for his portal because, having been accused of casting his *Bronze Age Man* from life, he wanted to prove by using figures much smaller than life-size that he could model a man or woman which could never have been cast. This reason is well known and no doubt true, but at first glance it appears superficial and neither bold nor original.[4]

It seems probable that he had other reasons. It was common for young intellectuals of the nineteenth century to find sin interesting and exciting, virtue drab and boring. That was as usual for them as to revolt against the bourgeois morality of their official society and church, and all the more because they had as a spokesman the inspired Baudelaire. In Baudelaire's words the aesthetic charm of the attitudes he championed could not fail to attract the artist-rebel Rodin.

From the moment he had made his choice, and not only from the time he was commissioned, all Rodin's drawings, which he did not bother to date or to sign, were an exploration of form and composition for the benefit of those *Gates*. These belong to what is known as his Dantesque period.

Made frequently on school copybook paper, ruled then in blue just as today, his drawings from 1878 to 1890 involved two distinct techniques. Plate 2 is an example of the anatomical pen-and-ink drawings of men, more often than of women, shown in violently active postures that suggest Rodin's involvement with the passions portrayed. The resemblance between these and Michelangelo's pen-and-ink studies has often been noted; their resemblance to Leonardo's pen-and-ink drawings is still more striking.

Plates 3 and 4 show drawings of the second technique, which resembles monochrome painting. Here, outlined in pen-and-ink, black-and-white gouache – sometimes with a somber red giving an effect of carnage, or a muted blue adding mystery and depth – are laid on with a brush. Bourdelle evidently knew these drawings which he referred to in his article as "the black drawings, companion pieces of the Sistine Chapel panels." A large number of these drawings represent lovers: a man and woman, or nymph and satyr, in various attitudes of embrace.

In contrast to Rodin's later drawings, which he said were the *result* of his sculpture, all these earlier drawings were its preparation. Plate 2 is an example. In the upper left portion one sees a primitive sketch resembling the early clay and plaster models for Rodin's *Gates of Hell*. The most prominent feature of those early plaster models is the central cross, shown also in the tiny sketch within this drawing. Here one sees the exact point on that early version of his portal where Rodin planned to place this group.

After 1890, Rodin made no more drawings from imagination. Whatever drawings he made thenceforth were from life, which suggests (since he always longed to draw from life) that before 1890 he could not afford to pay models for his drawing. He always managed to pay them for his sculpture, however, spending in that way most of what he earned. But if money was available after 1889, time was lacking, and except for a series of life drawings executed during the summer of 1896, few Rodin drawings of any sort exist that are traceable to the last decade of the nineteenth century. Apparently there was a complete break with drawing at this time in his life when he was more than ever occupied with his monuments.

PLATE 3. *Nymph and Satyr*

"The earliest, the black drawings, companion pieces to the panels of the Sistine Chapel ceiling, are they well known?" – *Bourdelle*

Black and white gouache drawn with a brush on lined paper. In such drawings, Rodin experimented with the drama of light and dark areas.

Courtesy Rodin Museum, Philadelphia, Pennsylvania

PLATE 3

PLATE 4

3 | The First Meeting of Rodin and Bourdelle

I T WAS just when Rodin most needed assistant sculptors to help enlarge and carve his monuments, that he discovered Bourdelle.

The exact date of their first meeting has not been established, unless the following rather terse note of Bourdelle's establishes at least the year: *"Très peu fréquenté l'Ecole, quitté définitivement au bout de deux ans,[1] puis plus tard connu Rodin qui vint demander voir mon Léon Cladel."*[2] [Attended the Paris Beaux-Arts School very infrequently, left there entirely after two years. Then later knew Rodin who came to ask to see my Léon Cladel.]

According to this unpublished and undated entry in Bourdelle's notes, Rodin's first visit would have been no later than 1892. It was probably earlier, for although the city of Montauban commissioned Bourdelle's bust of Léon Cladel on his death in 1892, Cladel had posed for Bourdelle certainly several years before 1892. As Léon Cladel was also Rodin's friend, very possibly it was he who before his last illness brought Rodin to Bourdelle's studio.

But whenever it was that Rodin actually became aware of Bourdelle, it is evident that for years Bourdelle had been aware of Rodin. No French sculptor of his time, Bourdelle said, could escape Rodin's power of attraction, which dominated the whole art world.

If this attraction had not reached Bourdelle at the Beaux-Arts of Toulouse before he left there in December 1884, surely by his first week in Paris,[3] when any young sculptor would naturally visit the Luxembourg Museum, Rodin's *Saint John the Baptist* must have exerted that power over him. But it was a somewhat later work by Rodin that attracted Bourdelle so strongly that even after sixteen years he could still communicate the emotion it had evoked:

11 mai 1906

Je ne vous ai jamais quitté depuis le jour où je vous ai connu, et cela fut avant que je vous sois présenté. J'avais vu votre tête de femme au Luxembourg, j'étais allé à elle qui m'appelait de très loin, je ne l'ai pas vue, je l'ai sentie. Depuis ce jour j'ai tendu sans arrêt vers la Source que vous êtes.[4]

[May 11, 1906 I have never left you since the day I first became aware of you, and that was before I had met you. I had seen your head of a woman at the Luxembourg, I went to her who called to me from very far. I did not see her so much as I felt her. From that day on without interruption I have directed my way toward the Source that you are.]

12

The marble bust of Madame Vicuna was the work that had thus called to Bourdelle, and there he recognized the master he had been seeking since childhood. Even if he had to wait several years after that before actually meeting Rodin, the wonder of having then another such marble bust to recarve in his own studio must have equaled all Bourdelle's dreams. And when Rodin came to see that work, on September 20, 1893, what he said then was worthy of being written home to friends in Montauban:

Paris, le 22 Sept., 1893

. . . *Rodin venu avant-hier, a vu le marbre presque à la fin. "C'est trop bien,"* *a-t-il dit, "je voulais un simple retapage et je ne donnerai pas cela à mon amateur,* *je le garderai pour moi. C'est du Carpeaux, votre marbre."*

Mais, lui dis-je, donnez cela où la matière si endommagée m'a fait défaut pour *tout rendre du modèle. Vous m'en donnerez une bonne, mise au point, que je ferai* *pour vous.*

"C'est beau," dit-il, "je voulais que vous vous réserviez pour la pierre et vous *avez fait un Carpeaux."*

Mais, lui dis-je, je me prépare au contraire à la mieux sentir.

"Celle-là," me dit Rodin, "sera pour nous, nous la ferons avec amour."

Et nous causions – il me conte ses débuts si durs, on l'accusait de mouler sur *nature, et la stupidité, l'ignorance des uns, égalait la haine jalouse des autres – car* *un artiste discerne un moulage d'une sculpture comme un dessin d'une photo-* *graphie. Il a tourné dans l'atelier. . . .*

Je lui ai conté que j'étais très touché de ce que je venais de découvrir que *j'avais en la personne d'un jeune sculpteur pour qui je ne m'étais jamais dérangé* *cependant, un véritable ami, absolument dévoué – Il veut quitter son travail pour* *venir m'ébaucher une sculpture qui le passionne, il a pour ce que je fais une sorte* *du culte qui dénote, qu'il se trompe ou non, qui dénote un enthousiasme, un coeur,* *une âme d'artiste. Et enfin il est bon de trouver des hommes comme lui.*

"Ah!" dit Rodin, "comme c'est charmant cela. Oui," dit-il, "et comme cela *rassure et fait du bien au milieu de ce siècle de coeurs atrophiés!"*

Oui chère amie, c'est Emile Derre qui attend un signe pour venir aider celui *qu'il voit trop haut sans doute, mais que cela change et est bon, mon Dieu, de* *trouver une main chaleureuse!*[5]

[Paris, Sept. 22, 1893   . . . Rodin coming day before yesterday, saw the marble almost at completion. "It's too good," he said, "I wanted a simple recarv-ing and I wouldn't give this to my patron, I'll keep it for myself. It's like a Car-peaux, your marble."

But, I answered him, give your patron this one where the material was already so much damaged that there wasn't enough to permit me to make a full rendering of the model. You can give me another marble, correctly measured and pointed, I'll make that one for you.

"It's beautiful," he said, "I wanted you to reserve yourself for the stone and you've made a Carpeaux!"

On the contrary, I told him, here I am preparing myself to have a truer feeling for the stone.

"That one," Rodin said to me, "will be for us, we will make it with love."

And we chatted – he described his early struggles to me – how he had been accused of casting his figures from life and how the ignorance of some outdid the jealous hatred of others – for of course an artist recognizes a cast from a piece of sculpture as surely as a drawing from a photograph. He paced about the studio. . . .

I told him how touched I was at having just discovered that I had a true and absolutely devoted friend in the person of a young sculptor whom I'd never gone out of my way to help. He wants to leave his own work to come and block out one of my sculptures which passionately interests him. He has a sort of veneration for what I am doing which denotes, however mistaken he may be – which reveals an enthusiasm that comes from the heart and the soul of an artist. And in fact it is good to find such men as he.

"Ah!" said Rodin, "how delightful that is! Yes," he said, "and how it reassures one and does one good in these times of atrophied hearts!"

Yes, *chère amie*, it is Emile Derre who awaits a sign from me to come and help me to whom he no doubt looks up to too much, but what a change that is, and Lord, how good to find a truly warm handclasp!]

Inevitably their sculpture had brought them together, and, from the letter above, so revealing of their temperaments, one sees mutual confidence already established. Bourdelle had become one of Rodin's *praticiens*, one of perhaps ten younger sculptors who helped him with transposing his plaster models into stone, or with enlarging and reducing his clay models. Judging from the letters, Bourdelle was first among all such assistants both in Rodin's affection and in his professional esteem. As to Bourdelle's feelings for Rodin at that time, Judith Cladel reports:

He spoke swept on by enthusiasm, the words in his quercynol accent rolled from his lips with the sound of rolling rocks. From six o'clock to midnight he held forth upon a single subject: *Rodin.* Never lover celebrated his mistress with a flame more intense than this disciple his master.[6]

Bourdelle's collaboration with Rodin's sculpture had prospered for eight years when a new shared interest brought fresh inspiration to their relationship.

PLATE 5. *Male Cambodian Dancer*

"There are certain very ancient stones whose historical period can no longer be told, and when one sees them, one is carried back thousands of years – then suddenly living Nature gives us the same thing. These Cambodian dancers have brought us all that antiquity can contain, their ancient art which is worthy of our own. We have just lived three days of three thousand years ago." – *Rodin*

Pencil and watercolor. Two flesh tones and a crimson costume.

The Fogg Art Museum, Harvard University

PLATE 5

PLATE 6

4 | Rodin's Crisis in 1900

BY 1900, Rodin had undergone five trials-by-fire in connection with his major monuments. His *Age of Bronze, St. John the Baptist, Gates of Hell, Burghers of Calais* and *Balzac* were desperate grapplings with his own passions, with his art and with a hostile public. By the century's end his *Bronze Age* and *St. John* had risen triumphant from such battles; for his *Burghers* he had accepted a compromise; but the fate of his portal and of his *Balzac*, the first never finished and the second rejected, must have represented total defeat for him. Both, however, had won the esteem of an elite of art lovers, and their tumultuous history had served to increase his renown with a larger public.

Rodin emerged from these trials more than ever himself. With all his creations assembled now in his own pavilion at the Paris World's Fair, he found strength for a new beginning.

Bourdelle, in his late thirties, was at the threshold of his independent, personal contribution to sculpture; Rodin, entering his sixties with fifty years of drawing behind him, now made drawing an end rather than a means. In the drawings best known to Bourdelle, the renewal of Rodin's lifelong study of form was carried forward now to the culmination of his powers in the least ponderous of materials. He was free at last to make as many drawings from life as he pleased, not for the sake of any commission or future sculpture, but for the life to be captured.

If it is a truism that in art every major advance follows a crisis of some sort, on that score alone Rodin's late drawings could not be the natural sequence of his earlier drawings. Moreover, these drawings followed an interruption of nearly ten years. After bitter quarrels with the French government regarding his display at the Paris World's Fair, Rodin raised the

---

PLATE 6. *Nero*

"Rodin's mortal frame is the hard wood sheathed in rough bark, dark with moss, herbs and lichen. At its base it wears gravel, tiny flowers, roses whose thorns catch and tear, also slugs and creatures that cannot see the light." – *Bourdelle*

Over this whole drawing, made lightly with pencil, a wash of terra cotta is spread. There are yellow touches in the wreath and in the brown-black mass of the lower portion. The heavy pencil lines were added last, on top of the color.

The Metropolitan Museum of Art, New York

money to build his own pavilion and there, with sixty-two works of sculpture before him, he must have seen he had created a world, whatever its human flaws and limitations. His later drawings, coming after so long and violent interruptions, were not only an advance; they were a new beginning.

Since in Rodin's own view his late drawings were the *result* of his sculpture, his sculpture must be the indispensable preparation for understanding the drawings. Rodin was first of all supremely gifted with an intuitive feeling for inner impulses, or the subjective life of bodies. Admitting as a basis this gift, how was he able to catch and express that subjective life? In his small clay sketches and in his later drawings, how could he recreate movements from nature that had never been recorded or even noticed?

The answer is: by patience. Rodin's two moments of pause are the key, the technical explanation of his supremacy in gesture. Because he waited until his models had lost awareness of his presence, and because he waited a second time for his vision to mature, he caught the attitudes that bodies make when they are alone.

And was it also by patience that Rodin could mirror, in his modeled surfaces, that same inner life of bodies? What is the technical explanation of his supremacy in modeling?

With sculptors of all ages and countries, Rodin – and Bourdelle also – shared the knowledge of form as a three-sided pyramid having one side in light, one in shadow and one in half-shadow, *demi-teinte*. It was above all in the handling of these planes — the sides of the pyramid as they control the *demi-teinte*—that Rodin and Bourdelle understood the science or the mastery of form. But Rodin amplified his form, accentuating the declivities and building the protrusions over hundreds of profiles, first because that was his temperament, just as it was his temperament to work in obedient clay rather than resistant stone; and second, because his natural nearsightedness, as well as the time and place in which he lived, favored that development.

When he had assessed his accomplishments to 1900, Rodin, like many another great artist judging his supreme achievement, perhaps found a particular flaw. Perhaps he saw the amplification of his form carried to a degree that was detrimental to the whole structure. If so, there was still time to make changes in what for him must have been the *new* work of his later drawings.

In his early drawings Rodin had used the male figure almost exclusively and in violently active postures suggestive of the sculptor's own involvement. In his later drawings, according to Bourdelle, he never asked a male model to come to his studio. This is not quite true, as shown by the drawing of a male dancer (Plate 5) which was made during the summer of 1906, and by the very curious and suggestive drawing, Plate 6. This drawing, which Rodin entitled *Néron* – Nero – represents a plump youth who might be the young Nijinsky. Yet it is true that the vast number of all Rodin's late drawings do represent the female figure either singly, in couples or in threes.

18

Around the year 1878, according to Léon Maillard, Rodin began reading Baudelaire, and evidently he continued this reading throughout his life. Knowing his great sympathy for that poet, Gallimard commissioned him in 1888 to illustrate a copy of *Les Fleurs du Mal*.[1] This commission coincides in time with Rodin's dry-point engravings (Plate 7) which he learned to make during visits to London with Alphonse Legros.[2] Indeed, Rodin's illustrations of Baudelaire's poetry, by their very fine lines and cross-hatchings, resemble his engravings more than any of his drawings. As subject matter there is only one illustration representing women or girls who might be lovers. This is interesting because, if the sheer number of female figures among Rodin's later drawings was in fact evidence that Baudelaire inspired the theme of Lesbian love in his work, that inspiration took a remarkably long time reaching expression.

The two young girls (Plates 8 and 9) may indeed be intended as lovers. So at least Bourdelle thought of them, judging from his note quoted here as the caption for Plate 8. But whether or not Rodin so intended, their love is expressed without passion. One senses perhaps more expression of Rodin's own feelings in his earlier drawings of heterosexual lovers, for example Plate 4, and this despite his remark that here the pose is from Clodion.

In all Rodin's later drawings one feels aesthetic joy to be the ruling passion, the one most often conveyed. His later drawings of lovers seem to proclaim the beauty of sexual passions, rather than the craving or fear expressed in his earlier drawings. Perhaps he found sexual love more beautiful as expressed by two female figures than by those of a man and a woman – more beautiful perhaps because more distant.

Even during the most violent period of his youth – in the drawings for his *Gates of Hell*, for instance – there is no willfulness or judgment. As Anatole France pointed out during that summer of 1900 when Rodin's *Gates*, still in their unfinished state, were exhibited for the first time, Rodin's Hell is a Hell of suffering and of tenderness. There are no demons such as appear to the left of Christ on the tympanums of the cathedrals, no devils to tempt or attack these sinners, or from whom they might hope to escape: "The evil angels by whom these men and women suffer are their passions, their loves and their hates, their flesh and their thought. . . . Hell is the earth, it is human existence, it is the flight of time. . . ."[3]

Rodin's sinners are not willful; they are swept on in spite of themselves. While many of them suffer the result of their acts in the degradation of the flesh brought about by excess, others suffer simply from the law of time. And that suffering is the more pitiful because it is inevitable and less often understood. Rodin's Hell is a Hell of compassion, of suffering *with*, for the creatures of his *Gates* reveal he shared in the suffering of his time, and of all time.

As in those figures for his *Gates*, Rodin expressed tenderness and compassion in his later drawings. Here he portrayed emotions no less deep but without violence, not in contorted but in natural attitudes, even when the emotions expressed were anguish or longing (Plates 10 and 11).

Bourdelle had observed this new thrust to life of Rodin's genius from its earliest manifestation. All these drawings were, of course, less strange but still more wonderful to him after ten years of working beside Rodin, whose ideas and practice had taught him that their source was in Rodin's veneration of Nature and of Life.[4] And although these drawings appeared only at the turn of the century, and were unlike any others, Bourdelle knew they had roots extending as far back as Rodin's 1877 visit to Italy, for Rodin had written him:[5]

> . . . Michel-Ange, qui m'a appelé en Italie, m'a donné de précieux aperçus et je l'ai copié dans mon esprit, dans certaines de mes oeuvres avant de le comprendre. Une fois compris, j'ai trouvé qu'il était dans la nature (mouvement) et que je n'avais qu'à ne pas le séparer dans mes modèles pour y mettre de l'antique, que ce mouvement y était comme une chose naturelle et non comme un alliage que j'aurais introduit forcément; de là mes dessins qui sont venus longtemps après cependant, et où on retrouvera du Michel-Ange tellement naturel, que l'on ne l'y soupçonnera pas. Par une analyse que nous pourrions faire, cher ami,[6] on le retrouverait. . . .
>
> Puis je suis arrivé au naturel qui porte toutes les écoles dans son sein, fondues ensemble. Aussi mes dessins sont plus libres, ils donneront plus de liberté aux artistes qui les étudieront, non pas en leur disant de faire comme tel, mais en leur montrant leur propre génie et les excitant à leur essor à eux, en leur montrant l'espace immense où ils peuvent évoluer.
>
> Votre ami, Rodin

[Michelangelo, who called me to Italy, gave me precious insights and I copied him mentally in certain of my works before having understood him. Once having understood, I knew that what I had found in him (movement) was in nature, and I had only not to separate that in my own sketches in order to include there what is also in the antique. For this movement was there as a natural element and not as an alloy which I might willfully have introduced; from this my drawings derive, although they came much later and Michelangelo will be found in them in such a natural way that none will guess it. *By an analysis which we could make, dear friend,* he would be revealed.

Finally, I have attained naturalness which carries in itself all the schools molten together. Consequently my drawings are freer, they will cultivate liberty in the artists who study them, not by telling them to do as I do, but by revealing their own genius to them and by pushing them toward its full sway by showing them the immense expanse in which they may evolve.   Your friend, Rodin]

Henceforth all the letters between Rodin and Bourdelle, and especially those which speak of the drawings (like the one just quoted, which although undated, must have been written in 1905), show their relationship growing from one between master and disciple to one between equals. The following unpublished note, signed by Rodin but written by his secretary, Rainer Maria Rilke,[7] proposes one of the many meetings between the sculptors during which their friendship deepened: *"le 10 Nov., 1905   En vous remerciant chaleureuse-*

ment de votre lettre, M. Rodin vous propose de venir lundi matin; il se fera un plaisir de con-sidérer avec vous les dessins que vous ne trouvez plus au Salon d'Automne." [Nov. 10, 1905 Cordially thanking you for your letter, M. Rodin suggests that you come Monday morning; at that time he will be pleased to study with you the drawings that are no longer at the Autumn Salon.] One may believe that it was in studying together the misunderstood drawings that Bourdelle learned the heart of Rodin's principles. He learned this also, of course, by observation.

PLATE 7. *Victor Hugo*

This is a dry point of Victor Hugo, of the type that Rodin learned to make during a visit to his friend Legros in London in 1881, and which he continued to make until 1886. These engravings, which are made on copper, are often mistaken for etchings, which are made on a thin coat of wax. With engravings, there is no rubbing out; each stroke stays.

Victor Hugo would not pose for Rodin, but did allow him to make notes from the doorway of the room in which Hugo worked.

The Metropolitan Museum of Art, New York

PLATE 7

23

PLATE 8. *Two Young Girls*

"Two young girls, like two newly begotten fruit born on a single branch and longing to unite, wishing to be but one." – *Bourdelle*

Pencil drawing. This is a later drawing, even though it lacks color; Rodin continued making such pencil drawings, modeled by rubbing the lead with a finger tip, to the end of his life. Inscribed by Rodin: "A mon grand ami Bourdelle."

Photo Bulloz. Courtesy of the Bourdelle Museum, Paris

a mon grand a...
Bourdelle.
Auguste Rod...

PLATE 8

PLATE 9. *The Embrace*

"Nests there are where love trembles in soft laughter, and in the deep, dark forks of the branches are harpies whose arms end in terrible fingers." — *Bourdelle*

Pencil, watercolor, and touches of white gouache; light flesh tones, sepia and yellow in hair, blue-green and sepia around figures.

The Metropolitan Museum of Art, New York

26

PLATE 9

35

Aug Rodin

10.66.6

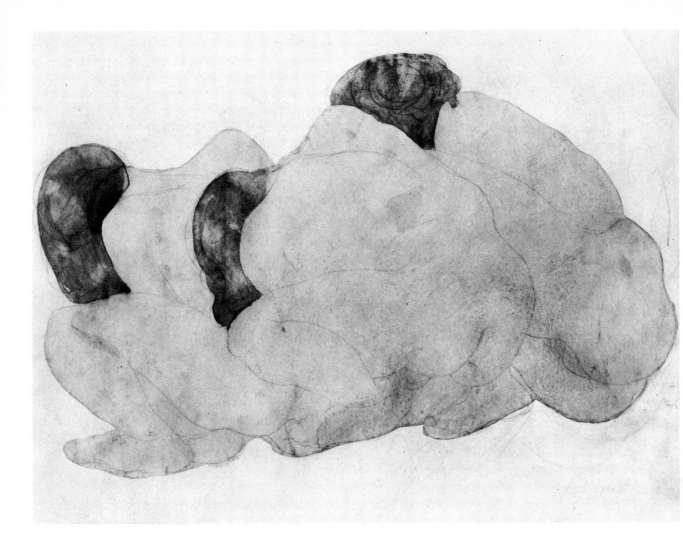

PLATE 10. *Three Boulders*

"This throng, this contemporary population, which seems to wish to tear itself from the maternal soil, you bring back into the stream, you return it to the vast horizons full of sky, in your drawings you re-adapt all to the rocks, the trees, the earth, to fire and to the excellent beasts." – *Bourdelle*

Pencil and watercolor; flesh tones and brown hair.

Courtesy Rodin Museum, Philadelphia, Pennsylvania

28

5 | The Method Found

MANY a summer afternoon Bourdelle watched Rodin in the garden of the *Villa des Brillants*[1] reading from the book of Nature, as he called his drawing from the model, or his quest for Life. Often Bourdelle heard him say there was no such thing as a drawing that is beautiful in itself, that the beauty of all drawing comes from the truth or the life it captures. As he would never impose his will in Nature's presence, Rodin never told his models what attitude to take, but watched them moving freely about, waiting for their unconscious gesture to recall some natural rhythm or contour, a tree perhaps or a boulder. And only when the principle underlying all natural form had fully merged with the vision before him, only when his mind had fully grasped that kinship, did Rodin's hand begin to move.

"Here the hand begins only when the mind has grasped the whole" – with these words from his article, Bourdelle signaled Rodin's first moment of pause which preceded the first gesture of his drawing. Then, holding his long pencil lightly and with his gaze still focused on the model, Rodin made his famous outline in one almost continuous stroke; and immediately he let the page fall to begin another. The pages he let fall now were no practice sheets but real drawing paper, usually ten by twelve inches.

Bourdelle said that drawings fell to the ground like autumn leaves from an ancient tree and were left in a trail on the grass when Rodin came into the studio, bearing perhaps only two. Such chosen drawings Rodin often covered with an empty page and held against the windowpane while he retraced his outline. And sometimes, either as the first or final gesture of his drawing, he expressed the massiveness by passing a brushful of flesh watercolor over the whole figure. Here it is important to stress that this color was applied either first or finally, because by looking closely at the drawings one sees it is sometimes laid over and sometimes under the penciled outline. In the drawing of Nero (Plate 6) color covers all the fine pencil lines, while the heavy pencil stroke circling the chin, face, shoulders and arms was made *last*, on top of all the color.

Although much of this description of Rodin's drawing method has been retold with variation nearly as often as these drawings have been mentioned, his important retracing, as Bourdelle reported it to his classes, has not been mentioned. That has been overlooked or ignored as though there were something disreputable about this step in his procedure, as if it detracted from the wonder of his drawings. But of course the end result is what matters in works of art, and wherever beauty is achieved, all the means are justified, and all become interesting. This perfectly honorable retracing is significant and observable in the best of Rodin's drawings.

Rilke may have been thinking of this step in Rodin's practice when he wrote: "Rodin's eye sees a great deal more during the sitting than he can carry out in time. He forgets none of it and often his real work begins after the departure of the model when he works from his well-stored memory." [2]

But Rodin's retracing had for purpose more than the improvement of contour as pattern or expression of form, and more than his memory was at work. One may believe this retracing was his second and most important moment of reflection, when he gathered up what he had seen and what he had understood to crystallize his inner and outer vision. As though to express what took place during that moment of crystallization, Bourdelle wrote: "All of Rodin's drawings are complete, even if they are not all finished. All have the sure grace of that which folds upon itself in order to open out full-blown."

Moreover, this retracing has a parallel in Rodin's sculpture, in his repeated use of the same figure placed at different angles with relation to the spectator on his *Gates of Hell*. Of this, the most obvious example is his "Three Shades," the three downward-pointing figures on top of those *Gates*, which are each the same figure, that of Adam, turned differently. On the *Gates* themselves there are many other examples, less obvious ones in which two casts of a single small figure – one turned upside down, the other right side up – express totally different emotions while answering one another like harmonizing opposites. Rodin worked as a composer over the orchestration of his *Gates*, and so, too, he composed his drawings.

Among his late drawings, Plates 10 and 12 each represent one model drawn three times in a single attitude, but drawn each time from a slightly different point of view. Plate 13, which Bourdelle likens to two beams of light crossing, is really two drawings. It is of the same model drawn twice but in two different poses, the two then fitted together to form this drawing, which is a composite.

The drawing of the beautiful incisive line, entitled by Rodin *Sommeil des Gorgones* (Plate 14), which resembles a Chinese character drawing, is one more example of his use of the same model and the same pose drawn twice. This drawing appears not to have been retraced. Evidently Rodin drew the figure on the right first, and, not satisfied, he overlapped that with his second try. The title one supposes to have been added afterward, as suggested by the drawing itself.

This drawing of the Gorgons, like Rodin's sculpture entitled *L'Iris*, must be among his works that were charged with obscenity. It is certainly one of the drawings most admired by Bourdelle, who mentions it more than any other in his notes and concludes: "*Ah, le lent effort conscient! L'analyse patiente! La science lente de Rodin, comme tout cela est en total ici! Ce dessin est sublime, il est une des totalisations de Rodin.*" [3] [Ah, the slow conscious effort!

The patient analysis! The unhurried science of Rodin, how all this is summed up here; this drawing is sublime, it is one of the compendia of Rodin.]

Later, in his article, Bourdelle defends this drawing and all such works showing the genitalia against charges of obscenity:

> Rodin is the great penetrator of human form. He studies that form without respite, even through garments which he always sees as espousing the body in action with beautiful folds. He uses drapery to accentuate forms and gestures, never to veil them.
>
> Rodin would never judge that there are in the human body parts that are beautiful and parts that are ugly, parts that are noble and parts that are shameful; and indeed he is right.
>
> If he were asked to paint the Last Judgment, he would shock in the same way and at the same level that Michelangelo[4] shocked. Then, when the vain noise had died away, his work would endure, just as Michelangelo's has endured.[5]

However, in his private *Notes*, referring to Rodin as a great tree, Bourdelle confides: "*L'arbre nombreux . . . travaille le plaisir de ses fécondités; ses sens avec effort projettent les branches de sa destinée, ses rameaux élancés sont désirs.*"[6] [This manifold tree . . . cultivates the delight of its fertilities; its senses strain to project the branches of its destiny, its wide-flung limbs are its desires.]

Of course, Bourdelle lost no time gathering up the scattered drawings which Rodin left on the ground when he came from drawing in the garden. And when Bourdelle reproached him for abandoning his masterpieces, Rodin replied: "*Laissez-les, ce sont des feuilles mortes; personne ne les veut.*"[7] [Leave them, they are dead leaves; no one wants them.]

This, although embellished by Bourdelle's epithet of the autumn leaves, is verification of Rodin's resigned attitude with regard to any true appreciation of his drawings. Evidently he did not expect they would ever be appreciated at what he and Bourdelle believed to be their true worth. All his contemporaries, if they mentioned these drawings at all, spoke of Rodin's reluctance to show them.

That reluctance, however, may have been simply the expression of Rodin's concern for these latest of his works. At any rate, it applied especially to his drawings made before the 1906 visit to France of the Cambodian dancers.

PLATE 11. *Despair*

"There are, caught by your art on these small leaves, clouds that harbor all human fears; there are the languors, the abruptnesses, the sovereign nobility of the dance; there are depressions and despairs, hopes and expectations. . . ." – *Bourdelle*

Pencil and watercolor on off-white paper; flesh tones, gray-black hair, upper background light blue; yellow, gray, and blue-green washes around figure.

The Fogg Art Museum, Harvard University

PLATE 11

PLATE 12

PLATE 13. *"Clouds"*

"Two women drawn together like two rays of light crossing. This drawing has such sureness, such breadth and fullness, the pencil flows over contours that are as pure as the curves of swimming fish." – *Bourdelle*

Pencil and watercolor; two flesh tones and a wash of blue-green. The figures are floating on a pale green sea. Drawing dedicated to Bourdelle.

Photo Bulloz. Courtesy of the Bourdelle Museum, Paris

PLATE 12. *Three Figures Under Water*

". . . the ones you recommence a hundredfold in meditation because they are the essential attitudes of human aspiration and they offer harmonious geometrical juxtapositions that parallel the great cosmic motions." – *Bourdelle*

These figures are water sprites deep beneath the surface of a green sea, swept by its motion. A wash of green watercolor completely covers these penciled figures, whose flowing hair is dark brown.

The Fogg Art Museum, Harvard University

35

PLATE 14

6 | The Cambodians' Gift

IT WAS for the Colonial Exposition at Marseilles that King Sisowath of Cambodia and his daughter Princess Samphoudry, with their suite of seventy-seven musicians and court dancers, came to France. As soon as they arrived at Pré-Catalan for their two Paris engagements,[1] Rodin hurried to see them. By the time they left, Rodin had become so entranced that he followed them back to Marseilles and took a hotel room near their *Villa des Glycines*, in order to make as many drawings as possible before they left France:

> *Je les ai contemplées en extase. Quel vide elles m'ont laissé! Quand elles partirent je fus dans l'ombre et le froid, je crus qu'elles emportaient la beauté du monde. . . . Je les suivis à Marseille; je les aurais suivies jusqu'au Caire![2]*

> [I contemplated them in ecstasy. What emptiness they left in me! When they were gone I was in cold and darkness, I thought they had carried away the beauty of the world. I followed them to Marseilles; I would have followed them to Cairo!]

Besides such joy, the ancient art of those very young dancers, whom Rodin called children, brought a new dimension to his drawing. Their art stimulated the growth of his own, bringing it to an unexpected flowering.

He gave his own account of his three days at Marseilles in an interview set down religiously word for word and published in *L'Illustration*. The interview is translated here just as it appeared in the July 1906 issue because, although it is not a document of the Rodin-Bourdelle relationship, it does reveal the development of Rodin's watercolor drawings, whose first apologist Bourdelle was. Moreover, Rodin's words here are a verification of all that Bourdelle wrote, not only of these drawings, but of Rodin's attitude to art in general. And finally, Rodin's description of the Cambodian dancers, and Bourdelle's article given further on, illumine one another equally.

PLATE 14. *Sleep of the Gorgons*

"Two female bodies, full, hard, solid, heroic scale, prostrate in the grandiose lassitude of sleep. Those four robust breasts risen like handsome hills in front of the chins. Expectation of furors, that which is to come, horror is there amid all that beauty. This calm drawing." – *Bourdelle*

Drawing inscribed by Rodin: "Près de l'autel. A. Rodin. Sommeil des Gorgonnes. Eschyle." Pencil and watercolor.

Courtesy of the Bourdelle Museum, Paris

There are certain very ancient stones whose historical period can no longer be told and, when one sees them, one is carried back thousands of years – then suddenly living nature gives us the same thing.

These Cambodian dancers have brought us all that antiquity can contain, their ancient art which is worthy of our own. We have just lived three days of three thousand years ago. Except among the Greeks, human nature is nowhere so perfectly expressed as in the art of these dancers. They have even found a new movement unknown to me: the staccato shudders that the body makes and in which it descends. And then, the great resource is that they keep their legs continually flexed; this permits the leaps which they can model as they will and grow tall at a given moment.

Another movement is peculiar to them, unknown in antiquity as well as to us; that is when, with arms spread, as on a cross, they simulate the motion of a snake from one hand to the other passing through the shoulder blades. In this serpentine movement, which belongs to the Far East, never seen elsewhere, the left arm describes a concave arc while the right arm describes a convex arc and, in the play of the arms, the flash of the movement goes out from the shoulder blades.

The flexed knees, also their own discovery, are a reserve of expressions because from that slight crouch they are able from time to time to build the body higher according to the rhythm of the music. Also the articulations of the fingers can be stretched and are very flexible; they have besides a tremor which is optional! Each single finger has its particular movement. The pulleys of the articulations are much more extended for the repetition of movements, and all are cultivated from childhood.

These are religious dances. I have always combined religious art with art; for when religion is lost, art is also lost. All masterpieces are religious, Greek, Romanesque, as well as our own French masterpieces.

This Princess (mistress of the Royal ballet) who looks so wicked, and this King* (her father) [see Plate 15], must be great artists, for without them all this art would disappear. The Princess is absolutely absorbed in the dances. There are many who make claims to beauty and who do not give it. The King of Cambodia gives us beauty. I am overwhelmed like Saul, thrown to the ground by an unknown light, the light that I have for so long studied in the antique.

From the point of view of form, these dancers are all admirably beautiful. Their faces astonish us. They recall our Italian models. There is a simplicity of modeling which also reminds us of the Egyptian granites. They could be carved in granite, highly polished, as pure as finely finished marble. But marble itself would not be as suitable, it would not render their forms as well as granite.

The masks are not grotesque and are nobly worn. Their costume, like all that is beautiful, does not hide a line. It seems one great complication, which it is not, for it allows the line of the nude to be seen.

The music is equally admirable. None other could accompany these dances. And the singer's slender, high-pitched voice which rises in the same key, does not slacken or hollow the line but rests suspended like a little swallow, intensified by the dull tamtam that punctuates the whole.

I am certain that these dancers understand and that they are capable of not falling down from the level of their superior art. There are great artists among those who direct them. The children themselves are very great artists. It's frightening!

This description of the Cambodian dancers is the verbal counterpart of the drawings Rodin made of them; here in his own words are the innovations that appear in his drawings from the time of their visit. Movements formerly unknown to him, and additional colors which their costume inspired, were immediately recorded in such drawings as shown in Plates 5, 16, 17 and 18. And the following reference to *la ligne* – "Their costume, like all that is beautiful, does not hide a line. It seems one great complication, which it is not, for it allows the line of the nude to be seen" – indicates the new clarity those dancers brought to Rodin's lifelong and most often repeated belief that a single principle of form unites all life and therefore all art.

This is illustrated particularly well by Plates 19, 13, 10 and 20 in which, besides the form of an individual woman, one may recognize the forms of a conch shell, of clouds, of boulders and of a peach. *"Comme nous imitons, ou plutôt comme nous sommes la Nature. Ces nuages n'ont pas plus de caprices que nous; nos âmes et nos pensées sont fuyantes aussi."*[4] [How we imitate, or rather, how we are Nature. Those clouds are no more capricious than we. Our souls and our thoughts are fleeting too.] Here the kinship of all Nature was not only observed according to its outward forms; it was also experienced in Rodin's subjective life. The Cambodians gave him a new revelation of that kinship. The line of their art, which the accompanying music and especially the voice of the singer did not interrupt or falsify, was the same as the line of the nude which the complicated costume did not hide. This was the "Great Line," defined in a letter to Rodin's young German friend, Helene von Hindenburg:

A definite line has been wisely assigned to all creatures; when they move within it, in obedience to their natures, they are incapable of ugliness. Even in the greatest throes of wrath a man does not swerve from the harmony of the Great Line. . . . When a woman combs her hair, the movement of the stars can be traced in her gesture.[5]

Because the brilliant costume of the Cambodian dancers did not violate the Great Line, it was worthy not only of appearing in drawings made from them; it also opened the way to the use of more color and to the use of drapery in most of the drawings Rodin made after 1906.

And the Cambodians' continually flexed knees Rodin saw as the technical explanation of the "readiness" which he admired in the best of Eastern sculpture, and by which, he said, Eastern art even surpasses the art of Greece:

> *Il disait: Les Hindous sont encore plus légers, plus élégants dans la proportion absolue. Les Grecs eux-mêmes sont plus lourds; et disais-je à Rodin: vous faites grand cas en art d'être léger, comme prêt à bondir? Certes, dit-il. La Beauté premiere est toujours prête."*

> [He said: The Hindus are even lighter, more elegant in perfect proportion. The Greeks themselves are heavier. And I said to Rodin: In art you attach great importance to being light, poised as though ready to spring? Certainly, he replied. Beauty of the first order is always ready.]

Some of Rodin's drawings of the Cambodians express that readiness to soar by his use of multiple outlines indicating the successive positions of the dancers' arms and legs. The flow of movement, the development of a gesture, is expressed more subtly in others, without recourse to multiple outlines. In Plates 5, 16, 17 and 18 Rodin solves the problem that had concerned him since, as a young man of thirty-four, he had tried to learn from Michelangelo how form might be used to portray life moving through time. But in these drawings Rodin surpasses his master, for by comparison with the movement here, Michelangelo's movement and gesture are hardly more than static contortion.

Rodin never carved the granite which he said would be most appropriate for the dancers; he is not known to have made any sculpture from them. But the hundreds of drawings he made of them, and most of those that came after 1906, are distinguished by additional shades of blue, yellow, green, red and violet in the drapery and sometimes in the background. They are known as *Les Aquarelles*.

But since additional colors are not the only new element of these drawings made after the Cambodians' visit, it is worthwhile to distinguish between them and their immediate forerunners.

Typical of the later drawings that Rodin made before 1906, are those shown here in Plates 13, 19, 21, 22 and 23. These are figure drawings without drapery whose penciled outlines are filled with a single flesh tone. Plates 13, 19 and 23 are seascapes, figures partly immersed or rising out of the sea. Plate 12 shows three figures under green water. A wash of

PLATE 15. *King Sisowath of Cambodia*

"This Princess who looks so wicked, and this King, must be great artists, for without them all this art would disappear. The Princess is absolutely absorbed in the dances. There are many who make claims to beauty and do not give it. The King of Cambodia gives us beauty. . . ." – *Rodin*

Pencil, watercolor and gouache; light ochre and sepia.

Courtesy of Mrs. Curtis O. Baer

PLATE 15

light blue-green spread over the lower half of Plate 13 indicates the sea whereon a tiny sail-boat and two female figures, named by Rodin *Nuages* – Clouds – are floating. The figure in Plate 23 is surely rising from water, which still falls from her in drops. She might be Venus or Leda, but in place of the swan is a plumed serpent.

Plate 19 is a Nereid seated on the seashore, one of her hands immersed in the shallow water, or immersed perhaps in the sand, for here the sea is not expressed by a wash of blue or green. Rodin made a series of such drawings representing nymphs of the Mediterranean Sea. Many of the drawings were made in Ardenza, Italy, during visits, beginning in October 1902, to Helene von Hindenburg, whom he called the last of his Nereids.

In his monograph Rilke wrote of these figures in seascape, and also of such drawings as Plates 21 and 22. Writing before 1903, Rilke said he knew drawings which had been trans-formed into terra-cotta statuettes by a brushful of deep ochre watercolor passed between their outlines. To this description Plates 21 and 22 correspond exactly. The first, which repre-sents a young girl carrying a water jug on her head, and whose form is modeled as in sculp-ture, might be a statuette from Tanagra, while the drawing, Plate 22, might be an Etruscan figurine. It is true that the drawing of the girl with a water jug is dated 1909, but obviously from the script, that date and the dedication were written simultaneously, in a single stroke. The date, therefore, refers not to the time when the drawing was made but to Mrs. Simpson's second visit to Rodin's studio. Since it was dated when it was dedicated, this drawing and probably Plate 22 also, may be from 1902, with those Rilke describes.

Typical of Rodin's drawings made *after* the visit of the Cambodians are those shown here in Plates 24, 25 and 26. These figures with drapery are the *aquarelles* proper, for which two and sometimes four colors were used. Rodin's color in these drawings is more often flat than in those made before 1906. It is seldom used to express depth. A finger may model the form which is outlined as before in pencil, while color is applied as in fresco painting, to de-fine the arabesque, the contoured mass.

Rodin, like Gaugin and Van Gogh (whose portrait of Père Tanguy he bought), collected Japanese prints. In the *aquarelles*, more thought is given to the silhouette which the pattern of the figure makes on the page, or the relationship between the filled-in and the empty areas of paper. It was in such designing of the whole page that the Japanese print-makers were supreme, and in certain of these drawings Rodin rivals those masters. Plate 25, for instance, recalls Hokusai and antedates Matisse.

But if the stylization of those painters meant the repetition of a symbol in shape or color, or any preconceived simplification, then Rodin was utterly unlike them. Each of his shapes is new because, as Bourdelle wrote, each was the result of an immediate observation of nature, and Rodin's simplification expressed his will to render only the essential.

All of which is not to say that after 1906 Rodin made always and only such drawings as these *aquarelles*. He was not always so lucky. And in fact he often went back to making pencil drawings without any color, such as the one shown in Plate 8. He also continued to make such drawings as Plate 27, using only two tones of sepia, and Plate 28, consisting of a single outline, but in which the design created by the enclosed and the empty areas is no less worthy of the Japanese. What can be said finally is that among the later drawings shown here, Plates 19, 21, 22 and 23 are typical of Rodin's later drawings before 1906 in that the form is often three-dimensional as in sculpture, while Plates 24, 25 and 26 show drawings that are typical of the greater number made after the visit of the Cambodians in that they often resemble frescoes or Japanese prints.

"The flexed knees, their own discovery, are a reserve of expressions [enabling them] from time to time to build the body higher according to the rhythm of the music. And the articulations of the fingers can be stretched and are very flexible. . . ." – *Rodin*

Black crayon over pencil and watercolor. The costume is orange-brown.

Courtesy of the Museum of Fine Arts, Boston

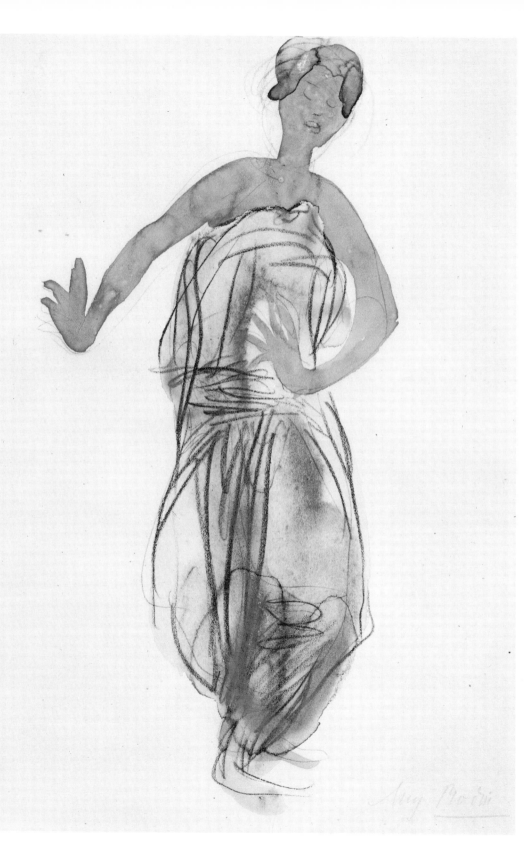

PLATE 16

PLATE 18. *A Child*

"When I was young I didn't see the beauty of children; I looked at their noses, their lips, their expressions. I was a dunce. One must see the whole." – *Rodin*

Pencil on off-white paper; flesh-colored wash for the figure; orange-brown hair; pale yellow background; blue-green drapery. This very young Cambodian dancer describes with her arms the snake-like motion which fascinated Rodin.

The Fogg Art Museum, Harvard University

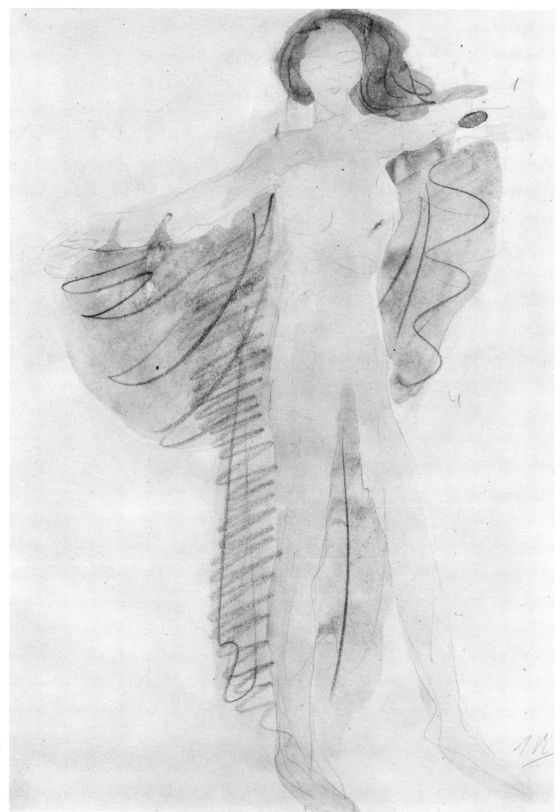

PLATE 18

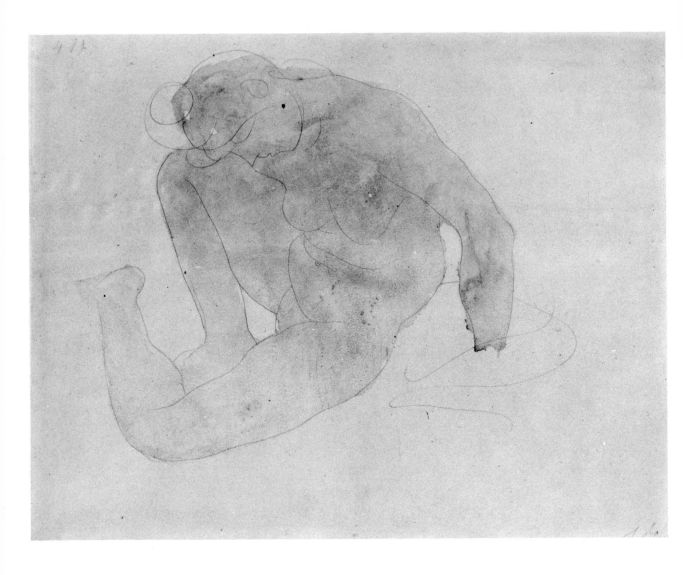

PLATE 19. *The Conch Shell*

"Here the hand begins only when the mind has grasped the whole." – *Bourdelle*

Pencil and watercolor on tinted paper; one golden flesh tone. This drawing of a nymph of the Mediterranean Sea has the beautiful wholeness which Bourdelle saw as the chief virtue of Rodin's later drawings and in which, he said, the drawings often surpassed the best of Rodin's sculpture.

Courtesy of the Museum of Fine Arts, Boston

50

7 | Rodin's Drawings Through Bourdelle's Eyes

MORE WILLING than for his others, Rodin agreed to submit his watercolor drawings to the hazards of exhibition. Perhaps the additional color made them more likely to succeed. At any rate, less than a year after the visit of the dancers, Rodin and the directors of the Bernheim Jeune Gallery had arranged to show during the following winter several rooms of drawings made, for the most part, during and after 1906. Elaborate plans for that exhibition were under way as early as spring 1907, for it was to be the first large showing of Rodin's drawings alone, that is, without any sculpture, and it needed careful preparation.

Notes, letters and the manuscript for one article, all at the Bourdelle Museum today and all focusing upon that exhibition, permit a reconstruction of events leading up to it.

M. Jacques Rouché's[1] offer to publish in *La Grande Revue* an article on Rodin's drawings to coincide with their showing recalls Rodin's undated message given at the beginning of this study. That undated message must also have been written in the spring of 1907, for one sees now that it concerned Rodin's choice of Bourdelle as author of the article for *La Grande Revue*. And Bourdelle's comment added to that message seems now to be directed at the famous writers who, although they were Rodin's faithful admirers, were not initiates of his later drawings.

Who were those famous writers? Surely the general misunderstanding of the drawings had begun with them; they were still writing as if the drawings were subordinate to Rodin's sculpture.

Even such a friend as Roger Marx wrote: "The drawings foretell and comment upon the works of sculpture," and Arthur Symons echoed him: "They are the drawings for the marble that take note only of the expression."[2] In short, despite the great admiration of these friends for Rodin himself and despite their sympathy for his drawings they still could not see them as works that needed no outside justification.

Other writers, not Rodin's friends, wrote what is always written and said of new works that make people angry by being unfamiliar. These wrote that a child could have made the drawings, that they were merely exercises, which Rodin himself was reluctant to show.[3] And during the winter of 1906 when Alfred Stieglitz opened his New York gallery with sixty drawings chosen by Rodin himself, Maurice Reynal reports: "It was not only the public, but the critics and the artists as well whose indignation was aroused."[4]

But apparently not even an ideal of understanding, plus the eloquence and good will of his writer friends, would have been sufficient background to introduce the exhibition. Rodin was looking for something more, or something else; otherwise, he might have chosen Rilke.

Although not yet a famous writer in France, Rilke had already demonstrated his understanding of Rodin's work. While Rilke's monograph on Rodin, published first in Germany in 1903, mentions Rodin's drawings only briefly (and of course only those made before 1903), his analysis of them proves that his understanding was then and is still today second only to Bourdelle's. Neither Rodin nor Bourdelle read German, and the French translation of Rilke's monograph was not published until 1928. It is reasonable to assume, however, that during the eight months Rilke lived at Meudon as Rodin's secretary, he would have given him a running translation of that work. But this was not essential; from their conversations alone Rodin must have learned the quality of Rilke's thinking. Something more, therefore, was in question.

That something more, which not even an understanding such as Rilke's could satisfy, must have been Rodin's wish to have his drawings explained in a sculptor's terms. Bourdelle's many letters, and his *Toast* delivered in Rodin's honor at a banquet in the forest of Vélizy, had proved Bourdelle's power of expression and, of course, his understanding. Bourdelle was not one to decline such an honor, not one to miss such an opportunity for expressing his admiration and, above all, not one to fail when asked to defend the cause for which he cared above all. Bourdelle naturally accepted.

He went first to lower Meudon to study the drawings at Rodin's house, usually known as *La Goulette*, but which Bourdelle in his *Notes* calls *La Coulotte des Moines*. This is Rodin's four-story house, bombed during World War I and now falling into ruin, but still bearing the plaque *Proprieté de l'Etat*. Here on the lower floors Rodin's casts, molds, drawings and various materials were stored, and here he sometimes retired from the activity of his other studios for a *cure de repos*.

In that house on the fourth floor, alone in what he described as a very beautiful room, Bourdelle looked at seemingly a million of Rodin's drawings. Actually, according to Judith Cladel, who spent more than six weeks in 1914 classifying the drawings stored at *La Goulette*, there were several thousand at that house alone. Evidently Bourdelle wrote to Rodin after one of his visits to Meudon telling him that the study had begun and asking the names of some of the drawings he had singled out. Rodin replied from a town east of Paris:[5]

18 Juillet 1907   Ille et Vilaine

Rodin, Fougères

Mon cher Bourdelle,
    Je suis bien heureux . . . [here two illegible words which seem to be "ce jour"]
puis vous donner des explications, écrivez-moi.
    Je ne sais, aussi, comment vous dire (le nom) tous ces dessins que vous voyez

sans moi, mais je sais combien vous êtes pénétrant d'une autre façon que moi. Ce qui fait que mes dessins et mes idées vivent d'une autre façon et sur un autre mode que celle que je pensais, ce qui les augmentente (de nouveauté et d'action pour moi). Non pas que nous sommes différents quant au fond; mais dans la manière d'exprimer. Car vous avez un feu que je n'ai pas, et qui vous a fait poète et sculpteur délicieusement fort.

C'est vous dire, ami, combien je suis heureux que mon travail soit échauffé du soleil du Midi, puisque vous me faites le grand honneur de parler de* notre art à propos de mes dessins.*

Ainsi est-ce une collaboration et celle à laquelle je tenais. Rien ne me tenais tant au coeur qu'à propos de votre ami vous disiez très haut notre commune profession de foi.

Je suis donc heureux de l'envolée que mes dessins vont reçevoir de votre esprit qui sait créer partout.

Votre ami, Rodin

[July 18, 1907   Ille et Vilaine   Rodin, Fougères   My dear Bourdelle, I am indeed happy [if I] can give you explanations, write to me.

I don't know either how to name all those drawings that you are looking at without me, but I know how penetrating you are and in another way than I am. This makes my drawings and my ideas live in a different way and at a different level and tempo than the one I had thought of, which increases their charm of newness for me and their power of action. Not that we are different fundamentally, but we differ in our manner of expression. For you have a fire which I have not and this has made you a poet and a sculptor who is deliciously strong.

This is to tell you, friend, how happy I am that my work should be warmed by the southern sun, in as much as you do me the great honor of speaking of *our art* with reference to my drawings.

Consequently this is a collaboration and one I have desired; nothing is dearer to my heart than that you should loudly proclaim our common profession of faith.

Thus I am happy about the flying start that my drawings will receive from your mind, which is able to create wherever it will.   Your friend,   Rodin]

Designed at least in part to tell Bourdelle what Rodin hoped the article would be, and to express his satisfaction with Bourdelle as its author, this letter, like other letters written to Bourdelle around this time and bearing such salutations as *"cher ami et collaborateur"* and the playful *"Mon cher Buonarotti grec et patron,"* conveys the congeniality of the two sculptors. It also clarifies the task Bourdelle had before him in writing his article.

Bourdelle's first step now was to make three long pages of notes, which refer to actual drawings. A translation of these notes follows.*

*A complete French transcript of these *Notes* is given in the Appendix.

18 juillet 1907   Env. 2. Collec. Toorpien

Rodin Fougères   Ile et Vilaine

Mon cher Bourdelle

Je suis bien heureux, que je
puis vous donner des explications
écrivez moi.

(le nom) Je ne sais aussi comment vous
dire tous les dessins, que vous
voyez sans moi — mais, je sais
combien vous êtes pénétrant et
d'une autre façon que moi. Ce qui
fait que mes dessins et mes idées
vivent d'une autre façon et d'un
(— Nouveauté pour moi et d'action) un autre mode. que celles que je
pensais, ce qui les augmentent. De —
sommes différents, quand au fond,
mais dans la manière d'exprimer,
car vous avez un feu que je n'ai
pas. et qui vous a fait poète et
et suppléant — — — délicieusement fort.

Rodin's Letter to Bourdelle from Fougères, Ille et Vilaine, dated July 18, 1907   (Facsimile)

After an absence of fifty years the original of the letter photographed here has come back to its first destination. As part of the Locquin-van Parys Collection of sculpture, paintings and written documents, it was bought by the French Ministry of Beaux-Arts and the city of Paris from the heirs of Bourdelle's first wife, and was returned to Bourdelle's studios, now the Bourdelle Museum, in 1959. This letter reveals Rodin's confidence and clarifies the task before Bourdelle.

Courtesy of the Bourdelle and Rodin Museums, Paris

NOTES ON RODIN'S DRAWINGS

In the drawings there is only the essential, there is nothing but beauty. A million drawings at the lower house called La Coulotte des Moines.† Drawings on the fourth floor in a very beautiful room.

Infallible observer of the least gradations, of the least gestures. Drawings like bolts of lightning – like the beyond of plastic Art. Torsos borne up toward the infinite – gusts from the eternal – root, human, divine and terrestrial – truth in a word, group of lovers, one sees Eden in this drawing.

❈

Odor of the human race.

❈

Tanagra-like heads.

❈

Nude women holding a tiger-skin.

❈

Nude woman holding at her side a trailing drapery, the whole resembling a lilac cluster or a frond of wheat.

❈

Nude of a young girl soaring, like the flight of an arrow.

❈

Drama of delight.

❈

Cupid and Psyche.

❈

Woman reading, a tender, silky drawing.

❈

The weight, the passion of the man carrying a woman on his back.

❈

Half-figure of a woman, torso drooping to one side, head resting on one shoulder, the arm extended and languishing like an autumn bough.

❈

Two young girls, like two newly begotten fruit born on a single branch and longing to unite, wishing to be but one.

❈

A woman, weeping, stands at the feet of another who is seated and calm; this drawing is as pure as spring-water flowing over a noble marble.

Two women drawn together like two rays of light crossing.

This drawing has such sureness, such breadth and fullness, the pencil flows over contours that are as pure as the curves of swimming fish.

❈

Anthems in the light. Flowers of science. Titan reabsorbing the sweat of his labor, reveals only his immortal calm where strays a motionless smile.

❈

Rodin today.

A tree of several shafts, a quiver of columns, a colonnade from a basilica or a temple.

A tree dominating all species nourished by the earth, all fruits, the bitter and the savory, watered by tears from the sky during the drama of storms, or colored, warmed and made downy by the sun's splendor.

Rodin's mortal frame is the hard wood sheathed in rough bark, dark with moss, herbs and lichen.

At its base it wears gravel, tiny flowers, roses whose thorns catch and tear, also slugs and creatures that cannot see the light.

The tree itself, the wood as it labors, plunges deep roots to breathe in the earth.

With toil and joy and with exquisite pain it drives the sap on high.

It suffers through its divers limbs, and in its many hearts, the caresses, injuries, thefts and benevolences of the changing seasons.

The somber bark and the wood, the alburnum that slowly, gently grows its circles to protect the multiple and quivering hearts, vibrate with infinite sensibility.

This manifold tree is meditative and may appear gloomy; it is sinewy and in its body struggle with the elements, it cultivates the delight of its fertilities; its senses strain to project the branches of its destiny, its wide-flung limbs are its desires.

Its wild arms full of clamor and wings of every sort, soar, writhing and interlacing with each other, in desperation here, in tenderness there.

Nests there are where love trembles in soft laughter, and in the deep, dark forks of the branches are harpies whose arms end in terrible fingers, knowing, agile fingers, obedient to orders, incessant orders

† [This must be another name for *La Goulette*, the only one of Rodin's houses having four stories.]

rise from the earth, orders from obscure foundations mount quivering to the boles.

And the passers by see only the bursting of buds heavy with sap.

Adorable foliage, more and more overshadowing and green as the commensurate powers that bring it forth are on the rise.

And here is the miracle, here is the fruit, a whole *harvest,* an *avalanche* of fruit.

❀

It is full-blown nevertheless, it is dazzling with bright dew from this side of the branches, it is violent and crimson on another bough, it is burnished and warmed by the sun at the highest reaches, all are essential.

Such is Rodin.

❀

Some of the loftiest of the sculpture, and all of his most worked-over drawings, are the ones that seem barely touched. These are the fruit of his supreme achievement, from his basket where one may eat divine fruit, his tree-basket where the fruit of the gods is heaped, peaches, crimson, rose, and gold.

❀

Drawing passed over the white page like a spike of wheat over a wheat field – when the grain is ripe and from afar Rodin, the harvester, cuts and presents it, it is for us to make our bread.

❀

Birth of Venus emerging from the waves like a bounding Triton, admirable drawing.

❀

Drawing bearing the title "next to the altar".

Sleep of the Gorgons.* Aeschylus)

Two female bodies, full, hard, solid, heroic scale, prostrate in the grandiose lassitude of sleep. Direct and simple foreshortening of the first plane, feet and legs bent, thighs wide open and drooping under the whole weight of sleep.

Abdomens and breasts facing the sky, backs absolutely flat on the ground, lower bodies to the fore, heads to the back of the drawing.

They each have the hand of the right arm supporting the head.

Their faces, wide, full, freely sketched, eyes closed, hair in large rebellious curls, are terrifying.

Those two elbows thrown back, overturned in sleep under the weight of the tremendously calm heads.

Those four robust breasts risen like handsome hills in front of the chins.

Expectation of furors, that which is to come, horror is there amid all that beauty. This calm drawing.

[Here two lines blurred, unreadable.]
with his epics.

Ah, the slow conscious effort! The patient analysis! The unhurried science of Rodin, how all that is summed up here; this drawing is sublime, it is one of the compendiums of Rodin.

❀

On the back of a letter.

Vigil-keeper, arms hanging crossed in back – the planes of the torso and arms are in projection – they are arranged by tiers in relation one to the other, in apparent chaos.

This drawing is terribly solid, it reminds one of a flayed and skinned torso of beef, everything stands out, each weight, each mass is demonstrated and comes forward – it reminds one of a hundred year old root, twisted by the years but indomitable.

❀

One of Sisowath's dancers draped in yellow, background grey and yellow, adorable little fresco.

❀

Young girl half standing, half-seated, the bust rising straight up full-face, arms along the chair, legs apart and falling, the whole forming a pyramid of unbelievable simplicity and completeness.

---

* [Greek goddesses, three sisters, Medusa, Eurayle and Stheno, who had the power to transform into stone all those they looked at.]

Observateur infaillible des ... des nuances, des moindres gestes.

Dessins comme des éclairs — comme l'au delà de l'Art. de plastique
torses soulevés vers l'infini. — Souffles éternels — ...
divine ... vérité en ... — ...

...

Peur de la race humaine.

...

Amour et psyché.

...

Le ... la passion de l'homme,
portant la femme sur son dos.

...

deux jeunes filles comme deux
fruits ... faits, nés
sur la même branche et
qui ... gémir qui
...

Une femme pleurant debout
aux pieds d'une autre assise
et calme — Cela est pur
comme ...

---

deux femmes rapprochées
comme deux ... qui
se croisent
Le dessin est si sûr
si ample si plein
le crayon y ...
que ... n'est pas
...

hymnes dans la lumière
fleurs de la ...
Titan qui ... ses
... ne montre que
son ... immortel
... immobile
...

Rodin actuel.
un arbre à plusieurs ...
faisceaux de colonnes de
basilique ou de temple.
Arbre multiple donnant
toutes les essences de la terre ...
tous les fruits, les amours
et les savoureux ...
des ... du ciel par le
... des orages, au
... velouté, coloré, ...
des splendeurs du soleil.
Les corps ... de
Rodin et le bois sont revêtu
d'écorces rêches et noires, de
mousses ... de lichens.
Il porte à sa base du gravier
des ... — des ... et
des épines ... et
... aussi, un tas
de ... qui ne voient pas
...
L'arbre, lui, le bois
... plonge ses
... la terre.

Il porte en haut ...
sous ... effort j'arrive
...
Il subit sur sa
... diverses dans ses
... multiples les
..., ... et les
..., les ... et
...
...
L'écorce sombre et
...
augmente ...
... protège la ...
...
d'une sensibilité infinie

L'arbre ...
... et peut paraît
... il est ...
... à corps avec
les éléments. Il travaille
le plaisir de sa ...
... avec effort
... les branches
de sa ... sa
... élancés sa
...
...
...
...
...
...
...

... il y a des nids ...
... tremble en
deux ... — ... de
... de ...
... il y
des harpies — ...
... bras, les ...
terribles, les doigts
..., ... aux

❇

Woman on her back holding in her two hands one of her raised feet.

General color tone flesh sepia, purity of form as of an egg.

❇

Admirable, Herculean Omphalos, masterful.

light pencil shadings

❇

Drawing entitled: The Song of Songs

Here is the whole supercharge of life, the intoxication of living.

This is a young girl, recumbent, who lets herself fall, who pours herself out like a branch of grapes from which the wine of the gods will cascade.

All, the contours of one sweep as bold and as pure in the conception of rhythms as a Greek amphora. The body tones golden, and the drapery crimson like the rusty crimson foliage of autumn.

The beautiful spray of grape-leaves that hangs over her, very near, like a luxuriant green cloud nearing an awakened land. This drawing is a marvel, it cannot be described, it has to be seen and one must suffer from loving it.

❇

The most intimate drawing.

A young girl seated, completely calm, completely nude, nothing in her hands, nothing at her feet, she is alone and she is legion, she is innumerable; she holds neither branches nor flowers, nor fruit, she has in herself all of these.

She is besides the wing that brushes the brow of men who are visionaries, she is a streak of lightning and the blossom of a peach-tree, she is one of its branches and she is the whole tree.

She is even the forest and the sea and love. She unlocks my hidden tears because she is beauty.

She gazes at me, barely golden against her white ground, she stirs not one of her lines, and yet, for me, by her very immobility she rocks the universe.

Why, oh God?

Why my fellows? Because she is art.

Bourdelle's Notes on Rodin's Drawings

One large sheet of paper, 11 by 17 inches, in quality comparable to our news-sheet, and the sort of paper Bourdelle preferred for his own drawing, is folded here making two 11 by 8½-inch pages. These Bourdelle covered on three sides writing with red ink the thoughts that came to him as he studied hundreds of drawings by Rodin, as he studied them now no doubt for the first time *in solitude*. Having watched Rodin at work, Bourdelle must have found many of the drawings familiar and must have known which ones Rodin loved best. But in these notes Bourdelle gave expression only to his own thoughts and preferences.

Unlike the other documents of this study which are also shown in facsimile, these hitherto unpublished notes have never left Bourdelle's studios from the day he brought them home following his last study trip to Meudon in August 1907.

Courtesy of the Bourdelle Museum, Paris

So end the three long pages of Bourdelle's private *Notes*, in which one overhears him speaking with himself of Rodin's drawings. They were apparently made at Meudon spontaneously but carefully, after long hours of study on several occasions. One imagines Bourdelle carrying his folded paper and his fountain pen[7] filled with red ink, making repeated trips from Gare Montparnasse to Meudon-Val-Fleury, to learn from seeing the drawings and to suffer from loving them.

These *Notes* are Rodin's drawings seen through Bourdelle's eyes, and seen until now exactly so by no other eyes; for Bourdelle never bothered to copy his *Notes*, much less to show them. Therefore they have been unread, even at the level of deciphering them, for more than half a century. Had Rodin seen them, he might have found the hopes expressed in his letter of July 1907 answered, and his drawings and ideas, warmed by the southern sun of Bourdelle's temperament, indeed live in a different way and at a different level and tempo than one he had thought of.

After describing and commenting upon the first fifteen drawings that attracted his attention, Bourdelle's thought turned to their source. The columns that follow, through the fourth paragraph of the second large sheet, are given to Bourdelle's intuition of the unseen forces blindly but cunningly at work in Rodin. Here Bourdelle uses the metaphor of the great tree to describe Rodin. Certainly he had not heard of Freud, nor was there at the time of his writing any such general vulgarization of psychology as today. Fifteen years after this section of Bourdelle's *Notes* were written they might have been referred to as his psychological or Freudian study of Rodin.

PLATE 20.   *The Peach*

"These are the fruit of his supreme achievement, from his basket where one may eat divine fruit, his tree-basket where the fruit of the gods is heaped, peaches, crimson, rose, and gold." – *Bourdelle*

Pencil and watercolor; four colors. This is the only drawing by Rodin in Bourdelle's collection that is dated; it is dated the year of the publication of his article on Rodin's drawings and was probably given in appreciation. Inscribed: "To my great friend Bourdelle, the great sculptor. 1908".

Photo Bulloz. Courtesy of the Bourdelle Museum, Paris

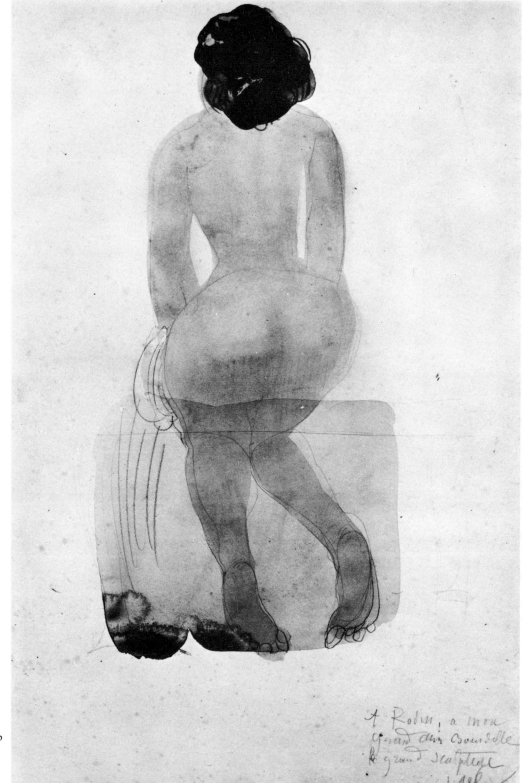

PLATE 20

PLATE 21. *Kneeling Figure with Water Jug*

". . . all the contours of one sweep as bold and as pure in the conception or rhythms as a Greek amphora."
– *Bourdelle*

Pencil and watercolor; two tones of terra cotta. The drawing is inscribed by Rodin: "To Madame Simpson, friend of my art since the first hour. 1909."

National Gallery of Art, Washington, D. C.

62

1842

à Madame H. Simpson amie
de mon art dès la première heure
Aug. Rodin 1909

PLATE 21

PLATE 22. *Birth of the Greek Vase: Study from a Kneeling Female Figure*
Inscribed by Rodin "Naissance du vase grec."

On cream-tinted paper, the penciled outline is filled with a wash of bright terra cotta; the dark strip at right is warm gray, apparently made on damp paper with some terra cotta in the brush. Because the body of a girl first inspired the form of the classic Grecian vase, Rodin reversed the process and could see in the form of such a vase the living body of a young girl.

The Metropolitan Museum of Art, New York

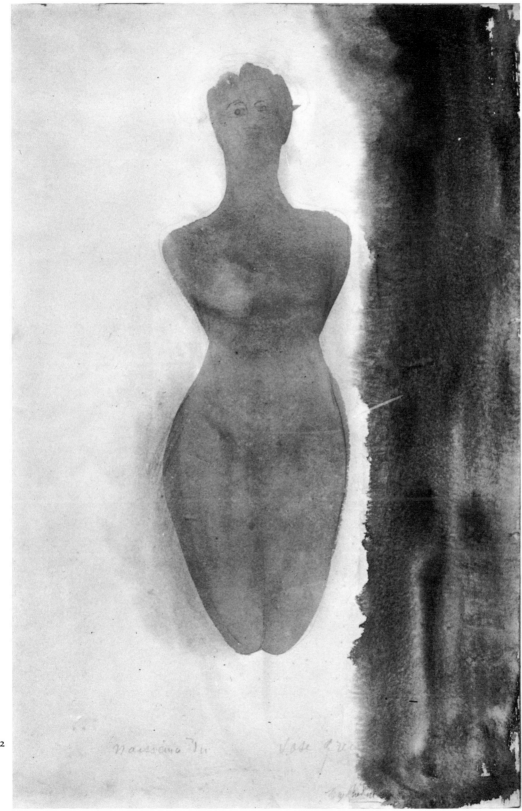

PLATE 23.   *Figure Risen from Water*
    Pencil and watercolor, with two flesh tones modeling the form, and a wash of blue-green behind the figure. The figure, risen out of the blue-green water which still falls from her in drops, might be Venus or Leda. But the wings behind her seem to belong to a winged serpent and not to a swan. It is at least certain that this is one of the drawings made at the time of Rodin's *Néréides*, in which the form is modeled by the flesh tones (1902–1905).

National Gallery of Art, Washington, D. C.

66

PLATE 23

8 | The Drawings in a Sculptor's Terms

BOURDELLE must have realized that his *Notes* were a private matter such as his article could never be, for there is no direct quotation from them in that more objective work. In his *Notes*, Bourdelle's delight in the drawings had been foremost. In his article the practical aim, to present the drawings in a way to show that Rodin the draftsman was as great as Rodin the sculptor, had to predominate.

Rodin's wish to have his drawings defended in a sculptor's terms had been conferred on Bourdelle years earlier. Rodin had given him the cornerstone of that defense in the now familiar phrase from his letter of 1903. By informing Bourdelle that the drawings were the *result* of his sculpture, Rodin had pointed to the heart of the general misunderstanding of their importance. Consequently, Bourdelle found it impossible to write of Rodin's drawings without writing also of his sculpture. There had to be an assessment of his accomplishment as a whole, and especially of his new beginning during the seven-year interim since the Paris World's Fair. Such scrutiny inevitably brought about self-examination for Bourdelle, as well as an examination of the general state of sculpture.

The Rodin-Bourdelle relationship had evolved according to the classic pattern and by 1907, Bourdelle was more than Rodin's disciple. As early as 1901, a year after his *Head of Apollo* had been left to dry and crack, Bourdelle discovered in that work his personal conception of sculpture made real. Soon after, on seeing the *Head of Apollo*, Rodin confirmed Bourdelle's belief by his remark, *"Vous me quittez?"* [You are leaving me?] This personal affirmation gave Bourdelle the confidence and perspective he needed to defend Rodin's drawings.

The more vigorous artists of 1907 had generally turned to other goals than Rodin's supremacy left to them. Even while the 1900 acclaim for his genius still resounded, younger painters had turned from the tenets of Impressionism, and younger sculptors from Rodin's vision. They were concerned now with the "integrity of form" rather than with the vibration of surfaces, with modeling or the fluency of light and gesture. By 1907, while granting Rodin never-to-be-equaled supremacy in those areas, sculptors gave new importance to geometric form and to the respect owed their materials. Suddenly there was a generation of carvers, or of those whose work was destined for wood or stone. These said that sculpture, to be executed in wood or stone, must be conceived in those materials and must be totally different *at the start* from any to be cast in bronze, even though all three might first be worked in clay.

New building materials and such structures as the Eiffel Tower posed new problems for painters and sculptors, as well as for architects. It was said that a work of sculpture should suggest a more durable habitation for whatever it might represent than the semblance of perishable flesh. And Bourdelle, who had discovered his ideal in the archaic Greek rather than in Phidias, and in the Romanesque rather than in the Gothic, spoke for his generation of sculptors when he said: *Il est temps de bâtir*[1] [It is time to build] – meaning, it is time to construct the work as a whole rather than to model the fragment.

There was, of course, no great living architecture in France such as the Greeks, the Egyptians or the Italian Michelangelo had known and to which their sculpture had been subordinate. There was the Romanesque, which had inspired Bourdelle's liberation from Rodin's vision. And there was the Gothic, which Rodin loved and studied as few of his contemporaries had done. But Rodin saw the Gothic cathedrals with the eyes of an Impressionist, as the drama of light and shade. He regarded them with nostalgia but as belonging to an art inevitably removed from him. Although he often expressed the melancholy thought that he might have been a better sculptor had he lived in the thirteenth century, the wonder of the Gothic had no such sway over him as the Romanesque had over Bourdelle. It could not empower him to change his life or his art.

Not only did Rodin not carve; all his works without exception were conceived in clay. It was now suggested that certain of his sculptures were still innocent of architecture even when translated into marble immortalizations of human flesh. And here once more the word "architecture" was used to mean the way the parts were put together to achieve wholeness.

In Rodin's later drawings, however, his intuition of inner impulses was as fully expressed as in his sculpture, yet displayed without detriment to the simple grandeur of the whole. This, as Bourdelle saw it, was the final advance of Rodin's art after 1900.

The handwritten copy of Bourdelle's article is translated here because it is more concise than the version printed in *La Grande Revue*, but especially because Rodin first read the article in Bourdelle's difficult script and it was to this version that he replied.[2]

The Drawings of the Sculptor Rodin
for His Exhibition at the Bernheim Gallery

At Meudon, on the estate that rises at the top of quarries,[3] in the galleries and studios of the sculptor Auguste Rodin, drawings under glass are to be seen almost everywhere; drawings washed with tones of color like projects for small frescos, still others barely touched with lead pencil.

Rodin exhibits these rarely and each time only a small number.

Very rapidly executed for the most part, these drawings are like flowers among the lordly works of the great sculptor, they are the tenderness of that hand which is practiced in the mighty and laborious task of statuary; they are like the fragile leaves that an ancient tree watches fall from its brow and unroll like a carpet at its base.

Not every one of these drawings has the full depth of the mind of this man, any more than each fallen leaf can tell the full grace and grandeur of the tree as a whole. But his quick harvest of forms, these drawings, are the great artist's repose and the reward of his labor. Here his smile is mingled with his effort and illuminates it. And these drawings, aligned like an army, gather up and summarize Rodin's whole and immense science.

All great forces are unique, and the repose of our sculptor does not resemble that of other men. To be refreshed, Rodin works and creates; ceaselessly he drives his thought to discover the countless ways of beauty. His halt is simply thought that finds.

These drawings are the result of the sculptor's long effort; in them, all the knowledge of art that he has slowly amassed is made tangible to the eyes of a few men.

Not many of these fragile leaves are gone over, corrected, or hesitated about. Here the hand begins only when the mind has grasped the whole. Occasionally the hand moves at the very moment when thought discovers.

All of Rodin's drawings are complete, even if they are not all finished. All have the sure grace of that which folds upon itself in order to open out full-blown.

They come to life before the eyes of those who understand them. They are always the expression of essential impulses. Now and then, outside their swift flood tide, certain ones rise laden with the perfume of perfection. Those are the drawings that Rodin has patiently nurtured. They are like troubled streams that ran through a furrow of earth which a seeker of clear water diverted to a clay bed, and of which he did not drink until all that was not clear water had come to rest at their depth.

So Rodin provides for certain of his drawings and these belong to the spirit alone, they have almost no other substance; or the substance born in them is simply beauty.

These elite among Rodin's drawings rise to the summit of his loftiest sculpture, they derive sometimes from quieter streams where all currents are reconciled.

They present, dare I say, the color of synthesis. They have lines of completeness, their conscious candor even surpassing the mighty constructions of this prodigious sculptor.

Rodin does not separate these tall stalks in his wheatfield; he does not reserve a sheaf of chosen stalks as he might well do. He has an equal love for his gropings toward the ineffable and the ineffable attained. He gives the public all, the ripe with the green wheat which will ripen tomorrow, to become our sweet-smelling bread.

For him, for us, the one contains the other; in thought we love to follow the phases of the growth of his wheat.

This pride, this quasi-disdain for those who are not willing to suffer a little in order to come to him, has often the effect that his work is little or not at all understood.

But there are those who know what Rodin is, who know the tremendous range of his art; and all that I write here is written for the joy of evoking the light of a great artist; it is written above all for the too rare joy of admiring.

I know there are many who grow impatient when Rodin is admired. And yet I must say, despite all that people have wanted to do to honor him, despite the flowers and the praises, Rodin is above praise or blame, which are indeed beside the point.

Too many times Rodin has been praised in a way that would defeat a lesser person. At such times even the desire to understand and to admire was barely present. And it was beautiful then to see Rodin smile and close his eyes while hearing himself praised for things which he holds in horror.

The fact is that the art of this man, like all that is lofty and powerful, remains a mystery. Even in his youth he was hard to deal with, and all the more because he was unknown. No one suspected the power that was in him, no one sensed he was being measured by that penetrating eye. In the crowd of men nobody hears the imponderable footsteps of isolated thought.

Rodin was still almost a child when he left the classes of one of the greatest of French sculptors, Barye. On long walks through the forest he meditated deeply on Michelangelo who, with the ancients, was his religion in art. Then, after persistent incursions into the structures of drawing (and there we find the great fulcrum), Rodin, when still a youth, had an extraordinary maturity, the maturity required to construct that splendid head of the *Man with a Broken Nose*. And further, the young Rodin had the unprecedented power to create that structure in equilibrium, so harmoniously balanced, which quivers beneath the thousand assaults of life — that grave figure of an adult called *The Bronze Age*.

This figure, *The Bronze Age*, was Rodin himself; it was his soul. And if I admit that there must be toil, and that everywhere, in surging up, life must defend itself, nevertheless, however enraged the fiery battles of art may become, no one has the right to deny the sovereignty of such works, which are an honor to art itself and to humanity.

These works, so proudly constructed, emanated from a mind which awoke to a consciousness of the immense field it was to encompass; this mind communed with itself in order to emerge and soar.

Rodin was destined to penetrate the heart of the human epic. He had observed human love and suffering, he had seen the heart's torment, the terror of the senses. Interrogation of destiny rocks his whole great work. Rodin, the man, has sometimes a loud, jolting laugh; but his work never laughs.

What constitutes a great artist is his power of linking the sensibility with which he is gifted to the slow and calm calculation of his science of art; it is his ability to remain master of apparently contrary forces and to be, still at this price, a sublime craftsman.

With a few other men I have the rare privilege of knowing the whole of Rodin's work.

To the poet, that work suggests ideas which are akin to it; to the storyteller it supplies numerous tales, but it remains above all a pure science of sculpture, the science of a sculptor gifted with an almost spontaneous personality, a personality that has been absolute from the very first of his works.

Every masterpiece contains all the other arts in power but unites them uniquely according to its own resources. It is indeed by the assembling of a seemingly unreal number of observations which relate purely with the laws of sculpture that Rodin is great. One could never repeat that often enough.

To appreciate him fully, one should know how to go straight to those examples of his work which summarize him. Otherwise it is necessary to try to comprehend the whole of his work at once. In Rodin's realm, he who does not select feels the grandeur of the parts without a sense of the whole.

When I had gazed into his soul, his past, his childhood, and his youth, which was so passionately devoted to his work, when I had paused before his adulthood and studied the portrait of this young man, when I had noted his bearing, the expression of his face with the feline power of a lion and the tenacity of an ox; when I had scrutinized this mask of lights and of shadows with its so concentrated smile, this gaze so youthful and already so much master of itself, then I understood the reason for Rodin's struggles. He is so entire, so much himself alone, that he must go on struggling.

How I would like to assemble a few of those who gather cobblestones to throw. I would bring them with me to Meudon, to the rooms where almost the whole of his achievement unfolds. I would lead them to the drawings, the portrait busts, the statues and the groups. Soon I would see them all shameful and grieving to have injured without understanding and without realizing.

Rodin is the great penetrator of the human form. He studies that form without respite, even through the garments which he always sees as espousing the body in action with beautiful folds. He uses drapery to accentuate forms and gestures, never to veil them.

Rodin would never judge that there are in the human body parts that are beautiful and parts that are ugly, parts that are noble and parts that are shameful; and indeed he is right.

If he were asked to paint the Last Judgment, he would shock in the same way and at the same level that Michelangelo shocked. Then, when the vain noise had died away, his work would endure, just as Michelangelo's has endured.

No part of any art is valuable solely because of its choice of subject. Works of sculpture have value uniquely as a result of the science of their planes, which govern their active parts and their parts in repose.

A drawing or a sculpture by Rodin progresses from the most subtle undulations of form to their union in the simple grandeur of the whole. This art advances from the fevers of the flesh to their geometric repose, and the first are so well enshrined in the second that their union is ineffable – ineffable by the sense of humanity which is equaled here by a sense of eternity.

I know very well that many will cry out against me in reading this study, this eulogy of Rodin, and I cannot help smiling in advance at their vain agitation, because I am certain that his work will live.

Do they even know how enormous that work is? Have they handled the clay, have they mingled their thought with it, or with the bronze, or with the marble, for thirty years? Have they dragged their hearts over the hurdle of our science as the artist has done in creating this sculpture which is so hard to capture, and so passionately loved?

For us sculptors, the struggle has to do with the beauty of the construction of planes and of values, be they made by the aid of clay, a pencil or a paintbrush.

We must establish our thought and utter it with our special resources. Our own language, as sculptors or painters, consists of masses in harmony with each other, of blocks in equilibrium containing and ordering their details, of weights rightly suspended with relation to themselves and to their neighbors; then, all this must be in perfect harmony with the surroundings, monuments, spaces, light.

In this proud domain of sculpture live shadows and lights which are beautiful only if obtained by the right concave and convex surfaces. And all of these we call the planes. But how many things are encompassed by that word!

When the exterior of the forms that we build emerges logically from its interior impulses; when a figure mingles with others without harming them, when on the contrary they mutually contribute to each other; when, besides their individual beauty, groups are conceived with an eye to augmenting the beauty of the neighbouring lines, in living harmony with them, then, when everything is interlocked as in a vast symphony, we artists bow before it because there we have a masterpiece. And if outside our own medium we sculptors decide to speak, if we agree sometimes to express in words what we are accustomed to say in forms, it is only out of love for a work, and in order to bring home to ourselves our own delight and rapture.

In his drawings Rodin gives us the royal privilege of seeing him at work; here he leaves visible the arrested moment, the emotion. Here he is willing to entrust himself to the public with his soul wide open. These white pages tremble forever with his spirit's emotion before the wonders of Nature. We seem to be looking at beautiful mansions whose plans have not been taken away; the stone cutters' models, the outlines, the scaffoldings, the tools, are still there; ready to be taken up by the workman's hand, they retain the noble attitude of work. We follow in the paths of the master builder's mind.

I write rapidly without rereading, my dear Rodin, because of your exhibition at Bernheim's. I write for those who have not seen the whole body of your work and because your drawings are exposed to so much scorn and misunderstanding.

I want simply to tell you the whole weight of beauty that I have always carried with me from your house. Ah, those vast rooms filled with your drawings!

The earliest, the black drawings, companion pieces to the panels of the Sistine Chapel ceiling, are they well known? And the ones that follow, simple line drawings made with pencil, or those stabilized by a single wash of water-color, or those covered all over with tones, and finally, those that have remained just as set down directly from nature, that master of the greatest artists.

The last are the most alarming to the public, the ones you recommence a hundredfold in meditation because they are the essential attitudes of human aspiration and they offer harmonious geometrical juxtapositions that parallel the great cosmic motions.

And those drawings which, besides the fundamental drama of their pure harmonious construction (a thing so rare when it is obtained not by being empty of all life, but rather by the fullness of all the living details subordinated to the entireties), comment upon the epics, literary intentions, symbols or rhythmic chants. And those that depict torsos above the sea, flights to the stars, crimsoned bodies that reflect the autumn; finally those that are like the shadowy apparition of destiny in the grey and blue semi-darkness. For you also use the sculptor's science of planes and of values to be a painter, and what a painter! A painter by the very foundation of all that constitutes the grandeur of painting.

There are, fixed by your art on these small leaves, clouds that harbor all human fears; there are the languors, the abruptnesses, the sovereign nobility of the dance; there are depressions and despairs, hopes and expectations. You have traced the features of love, the frenzied law of the sexes, the whole grandeur and the animal nature as well as the desolation of man, his most secret beauties of attitude, the whole law of the human body.

This throng, this contemporary population, which seems to wish to tear itself from the maternal soil, you bring back into the stream, you give it back to the vast horizons full of sky; in your drawings you adapt this multitude to the rocks, the trees, the soil, to fire and to the excellent beasts. The whole of life takes active part in the compendium of your achievement, and we are dazzled.

These last days, as I saw heaped before me again so much sculptural esoterism, or to say that more simply, so much knowledge of the laws that are the very inner life of our art, I thought: This century is made beautiful by your work, and the air would be less sweet to breathe without the power and grace it spreads abroad. I am certain that all artists, except those who are guided by selfish interests, or who hesitate or combat you without knowing you, would be happier and stronger if they might come sometimes to Meudon, to your Acropolis.

Seeing the greater part of your work assembled there one should not expect that everyone could appreciate the body of your powers as they are summarized in certain of your sculptures and drawings. And yet, some of your works do present you as a whole.

In a forthcoming study, I will follow you from your childhood; for as an adolescent you were already in pursuit of something immense that rose within you; then, when you were hardly an adult, you seemed like forests without boundaries, where innumerable collisions occur and thousands of wings are passing.

Ah, what a spectacle greets him who gazes into you!

For the moment, I would like to institute something like a pilgrimage to your museums, to your home, to your awesome achievement. For there is the church of genius, where the soul is restored.

I am convinced, my dear Rodin, that everyone seeing your work would pass from hostility to confusion and dismay, to attain knowledge and admiration at last.

ANTOINE BOURDELLE

In Bourdelle's *Notes* his delight in the drawings had been foremost. In the article, while that delight could not be hidden and although the metaphor of the ancient tree is repeated, the practical aim – to present the drawings in relation to Rodin's whole accomplishment in a way to show that Rodin the draftsman was as great as Rodin the sculptor – was foremost.

Although it cannot be affirmed that *all* the drawings used to illustrate this study are the same ones Bourdelle chose from among the thousands he had before him as he made his *Notes* and wrote his article, those from the Bourdelle Museum (with the exception of Plate 29, *A Fallen Angel*) are certainly his choice and those he was thinking of. For the rest, not even the drawings to which captions from the notes on the article are applied are definitely the ones he wrote about. And yet, these drawings *may* well be the very examples to which Bourdelle's comments belong.

Between 1910 and 1912, Rodin is known to have revised the whole of his *Gates of Hell*, and it was also in 1910 that he was posing for Bourdelle's portrait-bust (Frontispiece). Rodin is said to have refused this portrait of himself and to have broken off the sittings. Bourdelle called this his *Monument to Rodin*. It is one of his most personal and powerful works, but one made obviously more from memory than direct observation. It is less a portrait than a synthesis of all Bourdelle's thoughts and feelings about Rodin. Was it thus made by Bourdelle's choice rather than by Rodin's refusal to give additional sittings? Rodin's actual words in looking at this work were, *"Ceci sera peut-être compris dans cent ans."* [This may perhaps be understood in a hundred years.] Such words have been used as the highest praise and in fact nothing forbids the belief that Rodin gave Bourdelle his drawing of that period, *The Fallen Angel*, in appreciation for the bust. There are several fallen angels on those *Gates of Hell* and this late Dantesque drawing seems a reworking of the angel that lies entangled in drapery at the foot of the left panel.

The captions given in this present book are quoted for the most part from Bourdelle's *Notes* and from his article, or from Rodin's texts, or sometimes they are just bits of information. All are more useful not when fixed to this or that drawing, but as generally appropriate remarks, suggestive of perspectives through which the reader may wish to see this collection for himself.

By the subtitle of Bourdelle's article, and especially by the paragraph which reads: "I write rapidly without rereading, my dear Rodin, because of your exhibition at Bernheim's. I write for those who have not seen the whole body of your work and because your drawings are exposed to so much scorn and misunderstanding"[4] – it is obvious that Bourdelle expected his article to appear simultaneously with the opening of the exposition. However, it did not.

For that most important exhibition, where 219 drawings were shown (among which forty-three – or roughly one-fifth – represented Cambodian dancers), no complete date is available. The catalogue at the Bernheim Jeune Gallery, one of the few documents which were not confiscated from that gallery during World War II, mentions only the month and the year, but not the day of opening or closing

Invitation pour plusieurs Personnes
l'Exposition des Dessins de Rodin
Ouverte de 10 à 6 heures, (sauf les Dimanches)
jusqu'à fin Octobre 1907
chez MM. Bernheim Jeune & Cie, 15, rue Richepanse

whereas Bourdelle's article appeared in *La Grande Revue* of January 10, 1908, fully two months after the close of the exhibition.

The great success of the Bernheim exhibition is well known. For Paris at least, it marked the beginning of the period of wide popularity – if not full understanding – of Rodin's water-color drawings. It was followed by other exhibitions, several every year and in many countries, continuing up to and following World War I.

Less than two weeks after the Bernheim exhibition, Rilke was preparing a lecture on Rodin and his work to be delivered at the Heller Gallery in Vienna, where the drawings were also to be shown. (Probably some of the exhibits not sold at Bernheim's were shipped directly to Vienna.) Rilke wrote to Rodin from that city:

Nov. 11, 1907

You have nevertheless, dear and great master, penetrated further than you believe into the mystery of the Cambodian dances. Your insights, reaching back through the 18th century and through the Greeks, touch the definitive gestures of the Orient and evoke the sublime inscripion of the soul's movements which lift the weight from bodies that are blessed and artlessly docile. For me, these drawings were a most profound revelation.[5]

It is interesting that Rilke encouraged Rodin to believe in his Cambodian drawings even though there is no mention of them in Part Two of Rilke's *Rodin Book* written that same year. Rilke's admiration for the weightlessness of those dancers, which he ascribes to the soul's movements, corresponds to the lightness and readiness which Rodin saw as the chief virtue of Eastern art, by which, he remarked to Aurel, that art surpasses even the art of Ancient Greece.

Although Bourdelle's article could not have been widely appreciated, Rodin's delight in it, which spread in various ways and is established by many unpublished papers at the Bourdelle Museum, undoubtedly brought Bourdelle "un success d'estime." But Bourdelle's true sensitivity and genuine insights were hidden in his article, just as his authorship of them was hidden in the writings of men who later treated the same subject. It would be possible from this perspective to show that most subsequent critiques of these drawings restated Bourdelle's. All the insights of any value were there in essence.

This is not to say that everyone who later wrote of Rodin's drawings had first read Bourdelle's article or had heard him speak of Rodin – which he could often do more clearly than he could write – or that others merely clarified and enlarged upon his observations. Observations that are true occur spontaneously sooner or later to all true observers. But Bourdelle was the first to make observations with which later writers were credited. He made still other observations which are even now unappreciated.

PLATE 24. *Turbaned Woman*

"Half-figure of a woman, torso drooping to one side, head resting on one shoulder, the arm extended and languishing like an autumn bough." – *Bourdelle*

Pencil and watercolor; golden flesh tone and gray drapery.

Courtesy of the Bourdelle Museum, Paris

PLATE 24

PLATE 25

à Bourdelle Rodin

PLATE 26. *Seated Figure with Arms Crossed*

"The most intimate drawing. A young girl seated, completely calm, nothing in her hands, nothing at her feet, she is alone and she is legion . . . she holds neither branches nor flowers, nor fruit, she has in herself all of these . . . she gazes at me, barely golden against her white ground, she stirs not one of her lines, and yet, for me, by her very immobility she rocks the universe." – *Bourdelle*

Pencil and watercolor; one golden flesh tone.

Photo Bulloz. Courtesy of the Bourdelle Museum, Paris

82

PLATE 26

182 RUE DE L'UNIVERSITE

mon cher ami
Votre étude, de dessin qui
est un pendant à
l'étude de sculpture.
de Valery, pourrait
flatteusement pour moi
être en tête d'une édition
de mes dessins

Mais plus haut que tout
Cela, c'est de l'esthétique
vivante où les mots suivent,
et ne commandent pas,
car l'esprit y est comme
dans les livres de rigueur

Cela m'a fait penser à
un livre de foi.
L'imitation de Jesus Christ
pensée (de Spinoza)
((la connaissance de l'union
qu'a l'âme pensante avec la nature
entière. tel est donc la fin à laquelle
je tends.
acquérir cette nature supérieure,
et faire de mon mieux, pour que
beaucoup l'acquièrent avec moi))

((Si nous avons accompli quoi que
ce soit d'excellent, ne nous
enorgueillissons pas, à ce sujet
Cet orgueillissement est cause
que pensant être quelque chose de
grand, et n'avoir besoin de rien

182 RUE DE L'UNIVERSITE

de plus, nous restions au
point où nous sommes,
par où nous allons précisément
à l'encontre de notre
perfection))

Je reprend pour vous
ce sont des Psaumes ou
des quelqu'uns . C'est
toujours la synthèse qui
là, laquelle est trouvée à un
Côté de rigueur de la vérité
pousser jusque au nid des choses

Dites moi quel jour j'aurai le
plaisir de vous voir déjeuner avec
Madame et le jeune Bourdelle

et présenter à Madame
Bourdelle nos vives amitiés
Rodin

Je désire écrire ami mal que
vous en Calligraphie et
ami bien en substance

9 | "One Must See the Whole"

THE ideal contemporary reader for Bourdelle's article was of course Rodin himself, and for Bourdelle its real success was in Rodin's response, this personal letter of thanks:[1]

182 Rue de l'Université

Mon cher ami,

Votre étude de dessins, qui est un pendant à l'étude de sculpture de Vélizy, pourrait flatteusement pour moi être en tête d'une édition de mes dessins.

Mais plus haut que tout cela, c'est de l'esthétique vivante, où les mots suivent et ne commandent pas. Car l'esprit y est comme dans les livres religieux. Cela m'a fait penser à un livre de foi.

l'Imitation de Jésus-Christ
pensée (de Spinoza)

"La connaissance de l'union qu'a l'âme pensante avec la Nature entière, tel est donc la fin à laquelle je tends, acquérir cette nature supérieure, et faire de mon mieux, pour que beaucoup l'acquièrent avec moi."

"Si nous avons accompli quoi que ce soit d'excellent, ne nous enorgueillissons pas, à ce sujet. Cet enorgueillissement est cause que pensant être quelque chose de grand, et n'avoir besoin de rien de plus, nous restions au point ou nous sommes, par où nous allons précisément à l'encontre de notre perfection."

Je reprends pour vous, ce sont des psaumes m'a dit quelqu'un. C'est toujours la synthèse qui lorsqu'elle est trouvée a un côté religieux de la vérité poussée jusqu'au nid des choses.

Rodin's Letter of Appreciation for Bourdelle's Article   (Facsimile)

This unpublished and undated letter belongs to what may with equal appropriateness be called Rodin's period of great books and the period of his later drawings. For at the time of making these drawings Rodin was reading and writing more than ever before. He was correlating his thought of a lifetime with the wisdom of the greatest thinkers and was seeing each fact of nature, of art and of daily existence take its place in an over-arching whole.

No wonder, then, that he should respond to the moving event of Bourdelle's article in terms of those thinkers as well as in terms of his own deep thought.

Courtesy of the Bourdelle and Rodin Museums, Paris

Dites moi quel jour j'aurai le plaisir de vous voir déjeuner avec Madame et le jeune Bourdelle et présentez à Madame Bourdelle mes vives amitiés.

A. Rodin

Je désire écrire aussi mal que vous en calligraphie et aussi bien en substance.

[182 Rue de L'Université   My dear friend, Your study of the drawings, which is a companionpiece to your study of the sculpture for Vélizy, might, flatteringly for me, appear at the head of an edition of my drawings.

But above all that, it is a living aesthetic from which the words proceed and do not command. For the spirit found there is like the spirit in religious books. This reminded me of a book of faith.

The Imitation of Jesus Christ

meditation (by Spinoza)

"A knowledge of the union which the thinking soul has with the whole of Nature, such indeed is the goal toward which I strive to attain to that superior human nature myself, and to do my best that many may attain to it with me."

"If we have accomplished anything at all that is excellent, let us not take pride in it. Such pride causes us to think of ourselves as superior, and thinking we are in need of nothing more, we remain just as we are, thus we go precisely counter to our perfection."

I quote for you, these lines are from the psalms, so someone has told me. Here as always whenever a synthesis is found, it reveals a religious side of the truth pushed to the very nest of things.

Tell me which day I am to have the pleasure of seeing you for luncheon with Madame and the young Bourdelle, and please give Madame Bourdelle my warm friendly greetings.   A. Rodin   I would like to write as badly as you do in penmanship and as well as you do in substance.]

To Bourdelle this letter from Rodin must have seemed the greatest possible reward for all his work on behalf of the drawings. The warmth of his response indicates that Rodin was never too secure to feel touched by Bourdelle's true understanding, and his gratitude was expressed without delay.

The postscript shows that Rodin read Bourdelle's article in his difficult handwriting — therefore prior to its publication. This was to be expected, for Bourdelle naturally would have shown his article to Rodin as soon as it was written, and since he expected it to appear with the opening of the exhibition, it must have been ready before October. So the month and the year, September 1907, are indeed given and the enigma of the quotations, upon which an understanding of the letter depends, must alone have prevented its publication.

Rodin's letter testifies that the connection between his reading and his drawing, so obvious in his early imaginative work, was, in the case of his later reading and drawing, no less meaningful. Rodin denied having theories as he denied rationalism in art, although certainly he admitted to having beliefs and principles. By *l'esthétique vivante* surely he meant not a systematic theory but a lived commitment to art. He is saying that from Bourdelle's life devoted to art, true insights follow naturally with the air of detachment typical of religious works, and he names two such works that assuredly do not need to command and of which Bourdelle's article has reminded him.

In his youth Rodin is known to have experienced a religious crisis[2] and certainly his religious emotion was always strong. His friends knew *The Imitation* was one of his favorite *livres de chevet*, read surely during his devout childhood and reread from the perspective of the artist he had become to the end of his life. In later life Rodin compared the power of *The Imitation* to the power of a masterpiece. Indeed, in Rodin's thinking the two were simply one. We know he equated them for he recommended that book to Bourdelle as the ideal guide for a life devoted to art and explained that to experience it as such Bourdelle had only to read the word "art" in place of the word "God."[3]

Rodin's devotion was rather to the impersonal source of art and not to the apotheosis of man's genius most common to artists of his time, for he denied giving that genius godlike powers. Or if in looking at the cathedrals he was tempted to grant such powers to the men who had built them, immediately he corrected himself: ". . . *quel génie l'homme ne referme-t-il pas? puisqu'en collaborant avec le soleil il crée, lui aussi dans la mesure de ses forces – je demande pardon de ce blasphème, l'homme révèle mais ne crée pas.*"[4] [. . . what genius does not dwell in man, since by collaborating with the sun he creates, even he within the measure of his powers – I ask pardon for this blasphemy, man reveals but does not create.]

Yet it was not alone for the spirit of praise that Rodin admired and enjoyed *The Imitation*. He enjoyed it also for the virtues. Humility is the virtue set forth in the second quotation of Rodin's letter. This warning of the dangers of arrogance may be someone's summary or shortened translation of the lines from Chapter VII of *The Imitation*, beginning: "Be not proud of thy abilities or thy talents . . ." although the thought could also be Spinoza's or in either case, as someone evidently suggested to Rodin, a meditation of the psalms, which of course both Spinoza and the author of *The Imitation* meditated upon. But in any case we know Rodin's affection for such "homely" virtues and may believe it was the safeguard of his genius.

Judging from the physical traits of his letter in manuscript Rodin originally thought both his quotations were from *The Imitation*, but probably rereading brought doubts, and one plainly sees that he squeezed in the words "*pensée (de Spinoza),*" leaving the first title as written. This physical clue, like the mistakes in spelling and punctuation, indicates that he was quoting from memory a work thoroughly familiar to him.

The first quotation is indeed from Spinoza, from that early unfinished work usually translated as *The Improvement of the Understanding*, which Rodin surely read in Apphun's French translation.[5] Probably Judith Cladel had brought him this new translation, published one volume at a time between 1904 and 1908. There in Volume 1 on page 229, Rodin's quotation appears as the last phrase of one sentence and the beginning of another:

What is this superior human nature or character? We will deal with it in its time and will show that it is a knowledge of the union that exists between the thinking soul and Nature as a whole. Such then is the end toward which I strive: to attain to that superior human nature myself and to do my best that many may attain to it with me; *for it is also a part of my happiness to endeavor that many may clearly understand what is clear to me.*

Even at first glance the two phrases, given here within the two sentences to which they belong, recall Rodin's universal line. But to learn all they meant to him, and why he used them in connection with his drawings and Bourdelle's article, one should of course read Spinoza's whole essay as far as possible through Rodin's eyes.

It seems natural that Rodin would find his pantheism clarified by Spinoza's pantheism and his vision of a universal law of form carried to full conclusion in Spinoza's God of Immanence and Extension. But above all in Spinoza's fourth manner of understanding by which a thing is said to be perceived through its own essence, Rodin must have found the very manner not alone of perceiving a work of art, but of apprehending Nature from which such a work as one of his own drawings could proceed. Therefore he advised: *Regardons, ne préméditons rien, le destin choisit mieux; ne cherchez pas à avoir raison. Prenez garde que le chef d'oeuvre ait raison de vous.*[6] [Let us observe and presuppose nothing, destiny makes the better choice; do not try to be in the right. Take care rather that the masterpiece may be right instead of you.] Only in this way may a work achieve its own synthesis, or life, whose rightness when it appears eliminates all possible doubt.

Rodin wrote much the same to Helene von Hindenburg: "Do not be astonished if your drawings do not please you. You think they are without life, but Life comes as a reward for the time you have spent. It comes like a blessing when one has ceased to expect it. It is a work of longing which makes saints, and I might almost say which makes artists."

Finally, from his letter to Bourdelle, he made this comment on his quotations: "Here as always whenever a synthesis is found, it reveals a religious side of the truth pushed to the very nest of things." This is conclusive evidence that before using them in his letter or entering them in his notebooks, Rodin had found his quotations in context by a careful reading of Spinoza's whole essay as well as of *The Imitation*, both which he understood by the experience of his own work. When he retraced his drawing, enclosing the particular and the universal in the unity of a single line, at that moment of crystallization Rodin must have experienced "the thinking soul's union with Nature as a whole." So the sculptor's experience of a masterpiece and the philosopher's definition of a true idea are verified in each other, and if one asks for Spinoza's ideas in visual form, what more perfect answer than such drawings as those of Rodin shown in Plates 20, 25 and 26?

To Bourdelle personally this letter, with its quotations which pertain to their common *religion d'art*, told Rodin's happiness in being understood, and his happiness that Bourdelle's article should make clear to many what was clear to them both.

To a larger view the letter tells that while Rodin knew by the experience of his own art all that the greatest thinkers could reveal to him, he gained much more from their testimony than the realization that *tout se tient*. As Dante's work had provided a frame for Rodin's earlier thought and art, by such experiences as seeing the Cambodian dancers and reading Spinoza, that frame was extended and fortified to become toward the century's end, the structure Rodin needed for his late drawings and sculpture. Lacking such a frame of consciousness Rodin might have been no more than a supreme modeler of fragments.

When time had corrected his nearsightedness, it was his long experience of all the arts which permitted this full vision: *Quand j'étais jeune, je ne trouvais pas les enfants beaux. Je regardais le nez, la lèvre, l'expression. J'étais un ignorant. Il faut voir l'ensemble.*[7] [When I was young I didn't see the beauty of children; I looked at their noses, their lips, their expressions. I was a dunce. One must see the whole.]

PLATE 27. *Nude with Flowing Hair*

". . . from the most subtle undulations of form to their union in the simple grandeur of the whole, this art advances from the fevers of the flesh to their geometric repose, and the first are so well enshrined in the second that their union is ineffable." – *Bourdelle*

Pencil and watercolor on tinted paper. Three tones of burnt sienna.

Courtesy Rodin Museum, Philadelphia, Pennsylvania

PLATE 27

PLATE 28.   *Figure with Hands over Head*

"Drawing passed over the white page like a spike of wheat over the wheatfield – when the grain is ripe and from afar Rodin, the harvester, cuts and presents it, it is for us to make our bread." – *Bourdelle*

Ink on paper.

Courtesy Rodin Museum, Philadelphia, Pennsylvania

92

28

10 | The Heritage

FOR OVER thirty years Rodin was eclipsed from contemporary art. The turning away from his conception of sculpture, of which he had forewarning from the younger sculptors of his time, increased during the nineteen-twenties (the years of Bourdelle's mounting fame) and continued through the forties. Always known to be great, just as Michelangelo is always known to be, Rodin was no more thought of as an inspiration for living sculptors than that Renaissance master. His sculpture and his drawings were stored in the basements of museums if they were there at all (the Museum of Modern Art in New York acquired its first sculpture by Rodin in 1955).

It was the habit then to say that Rodin had ended a cycle. Art critics shook their heads over the evil effects of his genius. Bourdelle, on the other hand, was said to have constructed bridges reuniting the nobler past with the present and assuring a future for sculpture in the main architectural tradition – thus leaving Rodin somewhere beneath those bridges of tradition.

Bourdelle spoke of Rodin for the last time in public in June 1922, five years after Rodin's death. He spoke of him to the end of his days before his classes at the Grande Chaumière, but there Bourdelle spoke always as between confidants. So it was at the *Ecole du Louvre*, Pavillon Mollien, in one of a series of free lectures on art history that, from a manuscript which he entitled simply *Architecture and Sculpture of Our Day*, Bourdelle spoke publicly for the last time of Rodin.

It is characteristic, indeed inevitable, that the word "architecture" should be in Bourdelle's title. Architecture was more than ever in the air, as Le Corbusier's review, *L'Esprit Nouveau*, published between 1920 and 1925, spread throughout Europe. In a particular sense, Bourdelle had made that word his own, both by examples of his work and by his teaching. In his mode of expression it also stood for the order of the universe, for natural laws and their projections. An ideal architectural monument, in Bourdelle's conception, would be a microcosm of the universe; its angles and its planes would be an extension of those that support the worlds, and God himself would be a sort of architectural sculptor. And the reader of Paul Valery's Platonic dialogue, *Eupalinos ou L'Architect*, if he knew Bourdelle, seemed to hear his ideas and expressions quoted by Phaedrus from Eupalinos.

Bourdelle did not mention the pseudo-classic style of the Beaux-Arts in his lecture at the Louvre, but of Rodin he said:

Sauf en quelques éclairs splendides apportant le feu dans leur angles, sa forme éternisa la cendre de la chair.

Pénétrant, tel un dieu, le mystère intérieur des choses, il ne les soumet pas au destin de la pierre. L'art d'aujourd'hui et de demain ne suit plus ce chemin.

[Except in a few magnificent lightning flashes bringing fire in their forks, his form immortalized the ashes of the flesh. Penetrating as would a god to the inner mystery of things, he did not submit them to the destiny of the stone. The art of today and of tomorrow no longer follow that course.]

In thus predicting the future of sculpture, Bourdelle failed to foresee the art of a whole company of sculptors – several his former pupils – working at present on three continents and at whose hands "the ashes of the flesh" are a particular means of expression.

While all sculptors since Rodin are his heirs in a larger sense, of those today who use that element of his work to which Bourdelle refers above (but not in the sense that Bourdelle meant), the most justly renowned are Marino Marini, Germaine Richier[1] and Alberto Giacometti, the second Bourdelle's *praticien*, and the third a member of his classes at the time of Bourdelle's lecture. Rodin foresaw the art of these sculptors in the sense that he saw the need for extending his art to express, always in terms of the human figure but by the particular means of its transience, a counterbalancing, immaterial durability. This he accomplished in certain of his small clay figures, late torsos and late drawings (Plate 30).

In Marini's art the flesh is oftenest used to express total exaltation of body and mind, in Richier's art it is used to express terror, complete dissolution of the inner and outer being, while in Giacometti's art the frailty of the flesh is used most nearly as Rodin intended. The deepest kinship between Rodin and Giacometti is that each conceived for his art the seeming contradiction of making visible invisible parts of life. As Rodin explained to Helene von Hindenburg: "In my woman without a head I attempted perfection in my details and these should make you see the rest without its being materially there." Here of course it is not the woman's body that aspires to be whole but the work of art, and when that wholeness is achieved there are no missing parts.

To Helene von Hindenburg, Rodin wrote of the "perfection" of his details, but for him we know that Life was the only perfection. This is made clear by the quotation which Bourdelle gives:

Je connais deux plâtres de lui donnant tous deux l'identique et inévitable drame, la meme mêlée passionnée.

De ces deux corps de femme, aucun n'a la tête faite. Chacune tient en main ses pieds hauts, au niveau des épaules, leurs cuisses sont grandes ouvertes et comme écartelées, telles deux voluptés qui meurent sur leur croix.

95

*Et Rodin aurait dit: "La tête de ces corps? . . . que dites-vous? . . . vous êtes
bêtes . . . je vois . . . vous n'avez rien compris! Ce souci-là, ça n'existe pas, voyons!
Dans mon travail, elle est partout, la tête!* Faites tous vos morceaux vivants![2] Si
vous savez où est la vie des formes, le regard en suivant votre trame, reconnaissant
le choc de la palpitation venue des sources intérieures, fera que la pensée créera
toutes les parts absentes par le jeu des morceaux actifs."[3]*

[I know two plasters by Rodin both portraying one identical and inevitable
drama, the same passionate grappling.

Neither of these two female bodies has a head. Each one grasps her feet at
shoulder height, the thighs wide open and torn apart like two voluptuaries dying
on their cross.

And Rodin would have said: "The heads of those bodies? . . . what are you
talking about? . . . I see . . . you have understood nothing! That question is non-
sense. Why, in my art the head is everywhere! *Make all of your parts live!* If you
know where the living source of forms is found, the gaze that follows the warp of
your work will recognize the shock of palpitation coming from those interior
sources and thought will create the absent parts by the vitality of the parts that
are active."]

Certainly Rodin conceived beyond the material limits of his art, the very limits of which
many sculptors today are conscious. Thus whether one defines sculpture as Rodin defined it:
Le secret de la sculpture est dans le modelé, synonyme de la vie[4] [The secret of sculpture is in
the modeling, synonymous with life] or as Bourdelle defined it: *L'architecture est l'en de-
dans de la sculpture, et la sculpture pour valoir doit simplement la prolonger*[5] [Architecture
is the inward character of sculpture, and to be of worth, sculpture must simply bring that
out], the future of the art eluded prediction. The argument of Bourdelle's time, which concerned two approaches, has been abandoned now without being settled, for the reason that
both are true. The words "modeling" and "architecture" are not applied to sculpture being
made today which aspires neither to serve nor to be an architecture but seeks its own
autonomous laws distinguished from those of all the other arts.

The sculptor of today carries forward the search for what belongs essentially to his art
by looking back to its earliest manifestations in pre-history, as well as by looking as deeply
as possible into himself. He looks also of course at the world about him, and chooses according to his individual sensibility, between forms some of which are indeed new. He may
choose living forms which increase or decrease from within according to their own natures,
or he may choose those which cohere and are worn away by external influences, crystals and
the like, or numerical forms, which may be but are not always more spiritual than any others.
Or he may even choose from the world today man-made forms of the machine to reveal
whatever of beauty or meaning he finds.

And because man's sensibility does not change, but even among sculptors there are
predictable types of sensibility, and because art does not "progress," the basic opposition

goes on under the newer terms of "organic" and "constructivist." Only today it is generally recognized that whether a sculptor chooses the changing forms of life, or those which offer escape from all that is most uncertain and perishable in being numerically constructed, the choice is of subjective interest and not a matter to be settled one way or another.

Moreover, uniting all such preferences there is one aspiration belonging to every type of sculpture and indeed to all art, namely, the aspiration to wholeness, or in sculpture to the monumental, for in that art wherever wholeness is achieved, the work *is* monumental, the quality of wholeness in sculpture. And indeed it was just this quality of wholeness which made Rodin's late drawings superior in Bourdelle's sight to much of his sculpture.

Since the fifties Rodin's sculpture has risen from those actual basements and figurative bridges where for more than thirty years it was hidden, to stand firmly at the head of every catalogue and collection of modern sculpture. Today his work serves as a point of departure for critics and art historians who describe him as having *opened* a cycle.

Also Bourdelle, who seemed in his turn to be forgotten during the thirties and forties, has been reinstated since World War II. At his own museum in 1961, the one hundredth anniversary of his birth, a new gallery was opened where his monuments, too large for his other studios, are finally assembled.

But all the while throughout the contradictory appraisals of one and the other sculptor, Rodin's drawings have remained above the controversy, equally ignored by the general spectator, collector and critic during his periods of high and low favor.

For artists, however, Rodin was never in need of a revival, nor were his drawings ever less important in their sight than his sculpture. Even among so few as the present collection are examples which appear to have been sources for Matisse (Plates 25 and 28), for Picasso (Plates 6, 16 and 24), for Maillol's woodcuts that illustrate Daphnis and Chloe (Plate 26), as well as for the lithographs and paintings of Massilio Campigli's Etruscan period (Plates 21 and 22). These artists and others whose drawings do *not* resemble Rodin's (as Bourdelle's never did although he too made very fine but very different watercolor drawings), have received just what Rodin wished his drawings to give: ". . . liberty in the artists who study them, not by telling them to do as I do, but by revealing their own genius to them and by pushing them toward its full sway by showing them the immense expanse in which they may evolve."[6]

Hence there is justice in that Rodin's revival was started by the artists, started for English-speaking countries by Marini (on a visit to New York in the early fifties), by Henry Moore, Lipchitz, and the aesthetician, Herbert Read. And if today in his return to highest honor, just as during his lifetime, the fame of Rodin's drawings lags behind that of his sculpture, the drawings have friends nevertheless whose number may increase. For there have always been, ever since Bourdelle, some who see in these auroras of Rodin's autumn his vision of the whole manifested more clearly than in his mighty works of bronze and marble.

PLATE 29

PLATE 29. *A Fallen Angel*

Pencil and watercolor; three colors; inscribed by Rodin: *Chute d'un ange.* On Rodin's *Gates of Hell* are several fallen angels.   This drawing indicates his rethinking of that work and of the fallen angel lying entangled in drapery at the foot of the left panel. It was in 1910 that Rodin resumed work on his *Gates,* and that was also the year he posed for Bourdelle's portrait of him.

Photo Bulloz. Courtesy of the Bourdelle Museum, Paris

PLATE 30. *Torso*

"All of Rodin's drawings are complete, even if they are not all finished. All have the sure grace of that which folds upon itself in order to open out full-blown." – *Bourdelle*

Pencil and watercolor on tinted paper; two ochre flesh tones. Although the technique here resembles Rodin's late drawings before 1906, this was probably later because the simple inclusiveness as well as the pose recalls one of his last torsos.

Courtesy Rodin Museum, Philadelphia, Pennsylvania

98

E 30

Notes

Chapter 1. "Truthful Works Are Not Understood"

1. These two sentences – both Rodin's message and Bourdelle's comment – are written on one undated, 4 x 5-inch slip of paper filed with other previously unpublished papers at the Bourdelle Museum, 16 rue Antoine Bourdelle, Paris XV.
2. Quoted from Bourdelle's classes at *La Grande Chaumière*, Paris XIV.
3. From an undated letter to Bourdelle which Judith Cladel, Rodin's friend and chief biographer, places in 1903, *Rodin, Sa Vie* (Grasset, 1936), p. 356.

Chapter 2. Early Drawings

1. One small album of these drawings is at the Rodin Museum (Mastbaum collection), Philadelphia Museum of Art. Others are at the Paris Rodin Museum, 77 rue de Varenne, Paris VII.
2. Gustave Coquiot, *Rodin* (Bernheim, 1915), p. 46.
3. Léon Maillard, *Auguste Rodin* (Paris, 1899), p. 78.
4. Albert E. Elsen, *Rodin's Gates of Hell* (University of Minnesota Press, 1960), gives an interesting and thorough study of Rodin's reasons for choosing Dante's "Inferno."

Chapter 3. The First Meeting of Rodin and Bourdelle

1. In 1887, since he entered in 1885.
2. Poet and novelist of the region of Quercy (Languedoc), father of Judith Cladel.
3. January 1885, according to a letter to his parents at the Ingres Museum, Montauban.
4. The letter from which this paragraph is quoted has come back to its original destination, Bourdelle's first Paris studio, now the Bourdelle Museum. Bought and returned in 1959 by the city of Paris and the French Ministry of Beaux-Arts as part of the Locquin-van Parys collection of drawings, paintings, sculpture and written documents, this letter was published in *La Grande Revue*, November 1929, page 9, in an article by Ed. Campagnac.
5. This previously unpublished letter, which establishes for the first time the year and month when Bourdelle actually started carving for Rodin, is addressed to Mme. Marie Laprade, mother of Pierre Laprade, painter (1875–1932), to whom Bourdelle gave paints, brushes and encouragement.
6. *Rodin, Sa Vie*, p. 40.

Chapter 4. Rodin's Crisis in 1900

1. Republished with Rodin's illustrations by Limited Editions Club, London, 1940.
2. Painter and teacher at the Slade School, London, Rodin's friend since *La Petite Ecole*.
3. *Le Figaro* (newspaper), Thursday, June 7, 1900.
4. Rodin usually capitalized these words.
5. The important letter from which these paragraphs are taken is not at the Bourdelle Museum, although published with others of the Locquin-van Parys collection referred to above, in Ed. Campagnac's article in *La Grande Revue*, 1929.
6. Emphasis by Rodin.
7. The poet Rainer Maria Rilke was Rodin's secretary from September 1905 to May 12, 1906; his handwriting here has been verified.

Chapter 5.   The Method Found

1.   The *Villa des Brillants* was Rodin's residence outside of Paris from 1897 to his death in 1917, and there he is buried.

2.   Rainer Maria Rilke, *The Rodin Book,* trans. from the German by C. Craig-Houston (New Directions, 1960), p. 124.

3.   From Bourdelle's *Notes of Rodin's Drawings,* page 2, column 3.

4.   In Michelangelo's painting of the *Last Judgment,* the attributes of sex were shown. Pope Paul IV, after consulting with Michelangelo, commissioned Daniello de Volterra, one of Michelangelo's pupils, to paint the drapery which now covers those parts.

5.   These three paragraphs are from Bourdelle's article.

6.   From Bourdelle's *Notes,* page 1, column 3.

7.   Quoted from Bourdelle's classes at *La Grande Chaumière.*

Chapter 6.   The Cambodians' Gift

1.   July 1 and 10, 1906.

2.   Quoted from Louis Vauxcelles' conversation with Rodin printed in the catalogue of an exhibition of his drawings at the Devamberg Gallery, Paris, November 5, 1908.

3.   King Sisowath of Cambodia.

4.   Rodin gave Gustave Coquiot a collection of the tiny notebooks he habitually carried in his pocket. Coquiot transcribed thirty-two long pages of Rodin's notes in his book *Rodin à l'Hotel Biron* (Librairie Ollendorff, 1917). The note quoted here appears on page 63 of that book.

5.   The original French of this quotation cannot be given because the sixty-two letters Rodin wrote to H. v. H. between 1900 and 1914 have been published only in German translation: *Brief an Zwei Deutsche Frauen* (Holle & Co. Verlag, Berlin, undated publication). Although quoted in English in *Dialogues With Rodin* (Duffield & Green, N.Y., 1931), the letters have not appeared in French.

6.   Aurel, *Rodin Devant la Femme* (Maison du Livre, Paris, 1919), p. 168. To Aurel, French woman writer, Rodin lent twenty-two of his pocket notebooks from which she quoted in her book. Five such notebooks, 3 x 4 inches, are in the Mastbaum collection at the Philadelphia Museum of Art. Others are of course at the Rodin Museum in Paris.

Chapter 7.   Rodin's Drawings Through Bourdelle's Eyes

1.   Director of *La Grande Revue.*

2.   Léon Riotor, *Rodin* (Librairie Felix Alcan, 1927), p. 76.

3.   A. Ludovici, *Rodin, a Personal Reminiscence* (John Murray, London, 1926), p. 139.

4.   *History of Modern Painting* (Albert Skira, Editor), 1949, Vol. III, p. 89.

5.   Published in the article by Ed. Campagnac referred to above. Republished in *La Sculpture et Rodin, par Bourdelle, présenté par Claude Aveline* (Emile Paul, 1937), p. 112.

6.   Here Rodin refers to Bourdelle's southern origin.

7.   Bourdelle was proud to be one of the first to use a fountain pen for his drawings and always had it with him.

Chapter 8.   The Drawings in a Sculptor's Terms

1.   Quoted from Bourdelle's classes at *La Grande Chaumière.*

2.   The handwritten copy of Bourdelle's article covers two large 17 x 11-inch sheets of the same ordinary paper he used for his *Notes* of those drawings, but here the sheets are folded making eight 8½ x 11-inch pages on which Bourdelle's tiny script appears in purple ink.

3.   This describes the *Villa des Brillants,* above Meudon overlooking Paris to Mount Valerien. The quarries have disappeared now. The name of the villa refers to the lights of Paris seen at night like a sprinkling of diamonds. Most of Rodin's plaster casts are shown here in a large studio erected by Les Amis de Rodin in 1931 and may be visited each Sunday from April through October.

4.   These two sentences appear in the manuscript but not in the published article.

5.   *Rilke à Rodin* (Emile Paul Frères, Paris, 1931), p. 91.

Chapter 9.   "One Must See the Whole"

1.   This unpublished letter is also a part of the Locquin-van Parys collection at the Bourdelle Museum, but is *not* published in Ed. Campagnac's article. It bears the address of the studio given Rodin by the state for work on the *Gates of Hell.*

2.   Rodin was the only son of devout Catholic parents; his sister, a nun, died in 1863, and that same year Rodin joined the noviciate of the Fathers of the Holy Sacrament, where he remained for six months.

3.   Told by Bourdelle to his classes at *La Grande Chaumière.*

4.   From a long description of the Cathedral of Le Mans sent to Bourdelle for a book Rodin and Bourdelle planned to write together about the cathedrals and churches of France, quoted in *La Sculpture et Rodin,* by Bourdelle, p. 207.

5.   Spinoza, *Oeuvres,* Vol. I (Garnier, 1904). This is certainly the translation Rodin used; none other gives exactly this wording.

6.   *Rodin Devant la Femme,* p. 137.

7.   *Rodin à l'Hotel Biron,* p. 63.

Chapter 10.   The Heritage

1.   Germaine Richier died in 1960 but her art is still very much alive.

2.   Sentence stressed by both Rodin and Bourdelle.

3.   *La Sculpture et Rodin,* p. 188.

4.   *Rodin Devant la Femme,* p. 144.

5.   Bourdelle's lecture at the *Louvre.*

6.   Rodin's 1905 letter to Bourdelle.

French Transcript of Bourdelle's *Notes*

(First Page)

Notes sur les Dessins de Rodin

Dans les dessins il n'y a que l'essentiel; il n'y a que la beauté. Un million de dessins à la maison d'en bas, dite la Coulotte des Moines. Dessins au 4me étage, très belle salle.

Observateur infaillible des moindres nuances, des moindres gestes. Dessins comme des éclairs – comme l'au-delà de l'Art du plastique. Torses soulevés vers l'infini – souffles éternels – racine humaine divine et terrestre – vérité en un mot – groupe d'amants on voit l'Eden dans ce dessin.

❋

Odeur de la race humaine.

❋

Têtes tanagréennes.

❋

Femmes nues tenant peaux de tigre.

❋

Femme nue tenant à côté d'elle draperie tombante le tout aspect du lilas d'une gerbe de blé.

❋

Jeune fille nue comme envolée telle une flèche.

❋

Drame du plaisir.

❋

Amour et psyché.

❋

Liseuse dessin soyeux tendre.

❋

La faix, la passion de l'homme portant la femme sur son dos.

❋

Femme demi-figure – torse affaissé de côté, tête reposant épaule; bras étendu et languissant tel un rameau d'automne.

❋

Deux jeunes filles comme deux fruits nouvellement fécondés, nées sur la même branche et qui veulent s'unir, qui voudraient n'être qu'un.

❋

Une femme pleurant debout aux pieds d'une autre assise et calme – Cela est pur comme une source coulant sur un noble marbre.

Deux femmes rapprochées comme deux rayons qui se croisent.

Ce dessin est si sûr, si ample si plein le crayon y vogue par contours aussi purs que les courbes des poissons nageant.

Hymnes dans la lumière. Fleurs de la science. Titan qui résorbant ses sueurs ne montre que son calme immortel où *erre* un immobile sourire.

❋

Rodin actuel.

Un arbre à plusieurs fûts faisceaux de colonnes de basilique ou de temple. Arbre multiple dominant toutes les essences nourries de la terre, tous les fruits, les amers et les savoureux mouillés des larmes du ciel par le drame des orages, ou bien veloutés, colorés, tièdes des splendeurs du soleil.

Le corps mortel de Rodin est le bois dur revêtu d'écorces, rêches et noires de mousse, d'herbe de lichens.

Il porte à sa base du gravier, des fleurettes, des roses, et des épines s'accrochent, et des limaces aussi, un tas de bêtes qui ne voient pas clair.

L'arbre, lui, le bois au travail plonge ses racines il aspire la terre.

❋

Il porte en haut les sucs avec effort et joie, avec une ravissante douleur.

Il subit sur ses troncs divers, dans ses coeurs multiples les saisons, les caresses et les outrages, les larcins et les dons.

L'écorce sombre et le bois, l'aubier qui augmente lentement tendrement ses cercles protègent les coeurs multiples et tendres et vibrants d'une sensibilité infinie.

L'arbre nombreux est recueilli et peut paraître sombre, il est nerveux et dans son corps à corps avec les éléments, il travaille le plaisir de ses fécondités, ses sens avec effort projettent les branches de sa destinée – ses rameaux élancés sont ses désirs.

Ses bras farouches pleins des clameurs et d'ailes de tout ordre s'élèvent, se tordent, s'entrelacent désespérés ici, tendres là.

Il y a des nids où l'amour tremble en doux rires – dans des dards de rameaux profonds, obscurs, il y a des harpies – au bout des bras les doigts terribles, les doigts savants, agiles obéissant aux ordres,

ordres incessants du sol, ordres qui des bases, obscures montent en frémissements en craquements aux fûts.

Et les passants, eux voient seulement éclore les bourgeons lourds de sucs.

Feuillages adorables de plus en plus ombreux et verts à mesure que les forces qui les érigent sont plus amples.

Et voici le miracle, voici les fruits, toute une *moisson:* une *avalanche* de fruits.

❊

Ils sont pleins pourtant ils sont éblouissants de rosée et clairs de ce côté des branches, ils sont violents et pourpres sur tel autre rameau, ils sont dorés et tièdes de soleil, au faîte, ils sont tous essentiels.

Voilà Rodin.

❊

Quelques sculptures, les plus hautes, et tous ceux de ses dessins travaillés, ce sont ceux qui semblent à peine effleurés. Sont tous ses fruits suprêmes, de sa corbeille où l'on peut manger des fruits divins, son arbre corbeille où s'entassent les fruits divins, pêches pourpres, roses et d'or.

❊

Dessin passé sur la feuille blanche comme l'épi dans le champ – Quand l'épi est mûr et de loin Rodin leur[1] moissonneur le coupe et le présente, à nous d'en faire notre pain.

Naissance de Vénus   elle sort des flots en triton bondissant, admirable dessin.

❊

Dessin portant en titre ''près de l'autel''
Sommeil des Gorgones.
(Eschyle).

Deux corps féminins pleins, durs, solides, épiques, couchés prostrés dans le sommeil, lassitude grandiose – raccourci direct, simple au premier plan, pieds jambes repliés cuisses larges ouvertes retombant dans tout le poids du sommeil. Ventres et seins face au ciel, dos rudement à terre bas des corps devant, têtes au fond du dessin.

Elles ont toutes deux la main de leur bras droit qui supporte leur tête.

Leurs faces larges, pleines, largement esquissées, yeux fermés, cheveux à larges boucles cabrées sont terribles.

Ces deux coudes rejettés en arrière renversés dans le sommeil sous le poids des têtes formidablement calmes.

Ces quatre seins robustes en belles collines dressées au-devant des mentons.

L'attente des fureurs, ce qui va venir, l'horreur est là parmi toute cette beauté. Ce dessin calme.

[Four words missing here] et maîtresse avec ses épopées.

Ah! le lent effort conscient! l'analyse patiente! la science lente de Rodin, comme tout cela est en total ici.
Ce dessin est sublime il est une des totalisations de Rodin.

❊

Sur un dos de lettre. Veilleur, bras tombants croisés en arrière – les plans en ressauts du torse et des bras – ils sont étagés disposés les uns par rapport aux autres en chaos apparent.

C'est terriblement solide. On dirait un torse de boeuf écorché, tout est saillant, chaque poids, chaque masse est démontré et s'avance – on dirait une souche séculaire tordue par les ans mais irréductible.

❊

Danseuse de Sissowath drapée de jaune, fonds gris et jaune, petite fresque adorable.

❊

Jeune fille mi-debout, mi-assise, le buste s'élevant droit de face, bras au siège, jambes écartées et tombantes, le tout en pyramide, d'une simplicité et d'un plein inouis.

❊

---

[1] [*Le* moissonneur would be correct, but Bourdelle writes as above.]

(Third Page)

Femme sur le dos tenant de ses deux mains un de ses pieds levé.

Teinte générale chairbistre, pureté de forme d'un oeuf.

❊

Omphale admirable, herculéenne, dominatrice.

Légères ombres crayon.

❊

Dessin, titre : Cantique des Cantiques

Il y a toute la surcharge de la vie, ivre de vivre.

C'est une jeune fille qui, couchée, se penche, se verse comme une branche de grappes d'où le vin divin va jaillir.

Tout, les contours d'un jet hardi et pur d'amphore grecque conception des rythmes, les tons du corps doré et de l'étoffe pourpre, comme les feuilles rouille pourpre de l'automne – le beau rameau de feuillage de vigne qui pend sur elle tout près comme un nuage abondant et vert qui approche d'une terre en éveil, ce dessin est une merveille, il ne peut se décrire, il faut le voir et souffrir à force de l'aimer.

Le dessin tout proche : jeune fille assise, toute calme, toute nue, rien dans les mains, rien aux pieds, elle est seule et elle est foule, elle est innombrable ; elle ne tient ni rameau, ni fleur, ni fruit, et elle a en elle tout cela.

Elle est en plus le vol qui effleure le front des hommes, des voyants, elle est l'éclair, elle est aussi la fleur du pêcher, elle est une branche, elle est encore l'arbre tout entier, elle est aussi la forêt et la mer et l'amour elle déchaîne mes larmes invisibles parce qu'elle est la beauté.

Elle me regarde à peine dorée sur son fonds[1] blanc elle n'agite aucune de ses lignes, et, pour moi, de son immobilité elle agite l'univers.

Pourquoi, mon Dieu? Pourquoi, hommes parce qu'elle est l'art.

---

[1] [The final *S* is de trop as Bourdelle writes it above.]